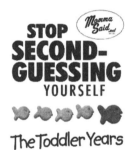

STOP
Momma Said...

SECOND-
GUESSING
YOURSELF

The Toddler Years

STOP SECOND-GUESSING YOURSELF

Momma Said.net
PRESENTS

YOURSELF

The Toddler Years

A Field-Tested Guide to Confident Parenting

Jen Singer

Health Communications, Inc.
Deerfield Beach, Florida

www.hcibooks.com

Library of Congress Cataloging-in-Publication Data

Singer, Jen.
    Stop second-guessing yourself—the toddler years : the field-tested guide to confident parenting / Jen Singer.
      p. cm.
    Includes bibliographical references and index.
    ISBN-13: 978-0-7573-0653-2 (trade paper)
    ISBN-10: 0-7573-0653-5 (trade paper)
    1. Toddlers—Development. 2. Toddlers—Care. 3. Parent and child. 4. Parenting. 5. Child rearing. I. Title.
    HQ774.5.S56 2009
    649'.122—dc22

© 2009 Jen Singer

Publisher: Health Communications, Inc.
      3201 S.W. 15th Street
      Deerfield Beach, FL 33442–8190

Cover design by Justin Rotkowitz
Interior design and formatting by Lawna Patterson Oldfield

For Nick and Chris

Contents

Acknowledgments

Thanks to Allison Janse, editor and visionary, who e-mailed me one day and said, "How'd you like to write some books based on MommaSaid.net?" Your clever insight, superb editing, and unwavering loyalty when, in the middle of the whole thing, I got cancer, will be forever appreciated. Thanks to everyone at HCI for making this book series possible.

Thanks to Wendy Sherman and Ed Albowicz for your guidance and friendship. Thanks to Robin Blakely for turning out magic, and for your continued support and love. Thanks, too, to Mark Stroginis for your work behind the scenes, and thank you to Jenna Schnuer who helped with the research for the book.

Thanks to my family: my mom and dad (aka Captain Red Pen), my brother, Scott, all of my in-laws, my nieces, and my nephew, Michael, who was a fresh reminder of the toddler years and its light-up sneakers and breakable items.

Thanks to my husband, Pete, for continuing to be my biggest cheerleader and my best friend. And to our kids, Nicholas and Christopher, who fill my days with joy and laundry.

Thanks to my doctors, Julian Decter and Alison Grann, who helped return me to health (and hair).

Finally, thanks to MommaSaid's community of parents who help make it a fun place to visit, and so graciously shared many fantastic tips and thoughts throughout this book.

Introduction

When I launched MommaSaid.net, my website for beleaguered moms who could really use a laugh, I had just survived the toddler years, but I was still reeling from the sleepless nights, potty-training setbacks, and toys and household items stuffed into the oddest nooks and crannies. I was relieved to find that other moms also felt as though the toddler years were a lot like Mr. Toad's Wild Ride: harrowing, yet often amusing, and always full of surprises.

Through the years, the MommaSaid community has generously shared war stories, tips, advice, and commiseration when it comes to those pint-size people we call toddlers, one- to three-year-old children who act a lot like little drunks: overly affectionate one minute, belligerent and incoherent the next, as they stumble toward the door.

Though it's been a few years since I was the mom of toddlers—with two of them under the same roof—it all came back to me when I watched my nephew, a toddler who is rarely still for more than a moment, do something none of the other kids in the family had tried: he picked up an ornately painted ceramic egg—the oh-so-fragile one from Germany—while we grown-ups all held our breath. "Ball," he announced. My sister-in-law tried to get to him, but *Blam!* He dropped it on the ground. He looked over the tiny pieces on the floor and said, "Broke ball."

And then it hit me: that's exactly the sort of thing that no one tells you about the toddler years, let alone what to do about it. I knew it was time to put together the kind of back-fence advice for surviving the toddler years that I've included on MommaSaid into one easy-to-read guidebook.

Here, I'll give you the big picture on parenting toddlers in a way that you haven't seen before. Throughout the book, MommaSaid's readers provide their own mom-tested tips that will prove handy when you're staring down a temper tantrum or trying to get your toddler to nap. It's like we're meeting at the proverbial back fence and, mom-to-mom, going through all the things that keep us up at night when it comes to toddlers, from tots who scale safety gates to that hideous shrieking noise your two-year-old has taken a liking to.

You might have a different experience with certain aspects of raising toddlers, and you'll no doubt have your own advice to give to friends who have toddlers now or whose babies are about to reach that first birthday, when so many changes begin. You're no doubt finding out that's when much of what a mom has already learned gets thrown out the window, likely along with a shoe and a sippy cup. (Go check. I'll wait.)

Whether every word is eye-opening or simply a reassuring pat on the back, remember one very important thing while you're parenting toddlers: you're not the only one going through it, no matter how lonely it feels at times. Whenever you need a pick-me-up, flip through this guide or drop by MommaSaid.net for laughs and validation. You know, just as soon as you dig your computer's mouse out of the toy box. (Go check. I'll wait.)

Been There, Done That

It was the scariest Halloween party I'd ever been to, but I was the only one who was frightened. I was wrangling my one-year-old, who had a poopy diaper trapped in a dragon costume with no snaps, in a public bathroom with no changing table. Outside the bathroom and across a stuffy room filled with children hopped up on Smarties, my unsupervised two-and-a-half-year-old, in a hard hat and overalls, was reaching for a plate of cupcakes smothered in chocolate icing. I realized then, *I've got* two *toddlers now*. One toddler had been tough enough, but two would surely kill me. Or so I thought.

Sweat poured down my back as I struggled to get my fidgety one-year-old out of his costume and onto the paper towels I had spread out on the grimy bathroom floor. I kept checking on my two-and-a-half-year-old, who was shoving his fingers into each and every cupcake, which had been placed at eye-level by some foolish mother who obviously had just one (freakishly inactive) kid to oversee.

By the time I cleaned up the poopy mess and rediapered and redressed my dragon, my little Bob the Builder was covered in chocolate frosting and rainbow sprinkles. So I hoisted my one-year-old up and carried him on my hip like a log, waded through the sea of children, grabbed my older toddler's wrist, and dragged him into the bathroom. While I was busy wiping the chocolatey mess off his hands, face, and hard hat, my younger toddler drifted away. Two minutes later, I found him playing in the toilet. I wondered aloud, "Does this party have an open bar?"

By the time we left the mothers' group-sponsored "fun-filled" Halloween party, I had silver glitter glue all over my brand-new olive-colored pants, a squirmy twenty-five-pound kid under one arm, two (still wet) painted pumpkins under the other, and a cranky kid who didn't like being corralled—by my feet—throughout the parking lot. When we got home, nap time was long over, even though no one had napped, and Trick or Treaters were already arriving at my door.

That was the day that I discovered that my baby wasn't a baby anymore—and that I probably wouldn't sit down for two more years at least. Soon I'd find out that whenever I took my toddlers to a playground, one would run in one direction and the other would run the opposite way, as though they repelled each other like two negatively charged magnets in fifth-grade science class. Meanwhile, I would run around in circles, trying to keep them from tumbling head-over-butt down the slide or from throwing my car keys down a drainage ditch while fiendishly giggling in my direction like a bad guy in a Batman movie or John Malkovich.

If you have a toddler, you know what I mean. When she was a baby, your kid, with her odd hours and inability to communicate that there's an irritating wood chip in her sock, certainly presented challenges. But your toddler? Well, she's something altogether different. Something that walks, talks, and relocates the bookmark you had placed in your novel last night to someplace you'd never think to look. Something small, but quick, especially in a crowded mall. Something that wants a hot dog and wants it *right now*! Something Momma never warned you about.

By the time you're speculating how to diffuse a full-out, knock-down display of Terrible Twos in the lobby at the local movie theater on a crowded holiday weekend, you're knee-deep in the toddler years, and all the sudden mood changes, sticky door handles, and "Get down from there!" frustrations that go with them. And boy, could you use a little help. I'll help you figure out how to handle them.

Gimme a break

Take it from me, the creator of *"Please Take My Children to Work Day,"* a rested mommy is a better mommy. That's why I've sprinkled these "Gimme a break!" messages throughout my book. Here, you'll find mom-tested tips for making more time for yourself, because after chasing your toddler around all day, you deserve a break.

Just a minute!

Life with Toddlers: The Game

START: Baby's first birthday

Your toddler takes first steps. Put down the video camera and move ahead three spaces.	Emergency room.	

Your toddler falls and bonks head on wood floor. Go directly to ER.

Your toddler says first word, "Momma." Move ahead two spaces.

Your toddler replaces favorite word "Momma" with dog's name. Move back one space.

Endure temper tantrum over jumbo pack of bubble gum in line at Target. Move back two spaces.

Toddler has fabulous new fetish: Putting away toys. Go directly to next coffee shop.

Find gooey mess on door handles throughout the house. Go back one space.

Toddler suddenly gives up pacifier with no effort on your part. Move ahead two spaces.

The penny you had spotted on the kitchen table is missing— and so is your toddler. Go directly to ER.

Coffee shop.

Toddler thinks like a cat: She climbs way up high on your furniture. Move back one space.

Popular new animated film is a rare Rated G! Go to movie theater.

Coffee shop.

Movie theater.

Mom of yesterday's playdate calls. Her kid's got strep. Move back one space.

Toddler keeps disappearing behind Daddy's chair to poop even though potty is readily available. Move back two spaces.

Coffee shop.

Toddler goes potty without coaxing, puppetry, or bribery. Go to finish.

FINISH: Preschool.

WE ASKED: How did you feel about moving from life with baby to life with toddler?

"First time, unprepared.
Second time, guarded optimism."

—*Julie, West Chester, Pennsylvania*

WE ASKED: What phrase would you use to describe the toddler years?

"Messy. Very, very messy."

—*Anne, West Milford, New Jersey*

Chapter One

When Your Baby Isn't a Baby Anymore
Transitioning to Toddlerhood

I knew exactly when my firstborn stopped being my sweet baby and started being my "No, Mommy!" toddler. It was the afternoon he took a chunk out of my shoulder.

One day after his first birthday, my son Nicholas had lunch at a restaurant with my mother and me. It suddenly became very clear that he didn't want to leave, because when I lifted him out of the high chair, he turned his head and sunk his teeth into me like he was on canine patrol, and I was a suspect on the run.

> **Okay, I admit it. . . .**
>
> "Life with a toddler is so much better. The baby stage doesn't include many rewards for cleaning up all the spit-up and poopy diapers."
>
> —*Whitney,*
> *Bridgewater, Virginia*

Up until that moment, he was mainly gentle and kind, not to mention obedient. For the most part, he went along with my plans. He never questioned my authority, and he often greeted me after nap time as though I was a revered celebrity who'd happened upon him in his crib. To him, I was the "It Girl" of the house.

But soon after he took his first steps, his kindly personality took a little detour. Before his birthday, he was fairly agreeable, easy to please, and a good eater. After his birthday, he ditched his baby food and replaced it with a penchant for Cheerios and not much else. He started yelling "No!" whenever I did something he didn't like, which, apparently, was more often than not. And he started running away from me, even though I chased after him yelling, "Mommy's pregnant. Slow down!"

It's not that I wanted him to be a baby forever. After all the colic, sleep deprivation, and lugging around that went with his first year, I was actually pretty darn happy to move on to the next stage of motherhood. I just didn't realize that the next stage involved biting. And kicking. And sprinting when I least expected it.

Whether your baby's first birthday is still on your calendar or you've already passed that date, no doubt you're dealing with the baby-to-toddler transition, and all the sippy cups, playdates, and mad dashes through parking lots that go with it. What's a momma to do?

WE ASKED: What were the early signs that your toddler was asserting his or her independence?

"Two words: 'NO MOMMY!'"

—*Jennifer, Flemington, New Jersey*

It's Always Something

THE BEST PART about toddlers is that they're always learning something new. The worst part about toddlers is that they're always learning something new. How can you possibly keep up? One minute, your toddler is playing quietly by herself. The next, she's putting your cell phone in the garbage can and fiddling with the screen door.

Some toddler behaviors are expected, like the ones you read about in milestone books. Others are unexpected, if not confounding and often exhausting for you. So what can you expect when your baby becomes a toddler?

"Dada. Dada. Dada."
Your Toddler's Growing Vocabulary

BY AGE ONE, your toddler might say a few words. She might even know what they mean. By sixteen months, girls can typically say about fifty words, and boys can say thirty, which explains why my son could simply say "boat" while his female playmate could say "Look, Mommy! It's a boat. It's a blue boat." I waited for her to give her dissertation on yachting, but it was circle time at our mom-tot class. Besides, my son was busy saying, "Boatboatboatboatboat" like Rain Man when he insisted on seeing *The People's Court*, repeating over and over, "Definitely Wapner."

You can help your toddler build his vocabulary by repeating words for him, pointing things out, and talking to him in that slightly irritating Mommy voice: "Open the door now, Zach. Open the door. Good boy, Zach. You opened the door! What a big boy for opening the door." Just remember to turn it off when you're talking to grown-ups, because the FedEx guy doesn't want to know he's a good boy for bringing you the pretty package.

Also, read to your toddler at least fifteen minutes a day. Ask her to point to objects on the page and try to get her to repeat the word, if she can, but don't pressure her. Make sure you praise her for using words, especially new ones. Some moms use vocabulary-building books and games or hope that *Sesame Street* will teach their toddlers a few words. I've found, though, that talking to your toddler all day works very well.

By her first birthday, your toddler should be able to say up to five words. Over the next couple of weeks, she might add a few words or sounds that she thinks are words, and she might even use inflection correctly. By sixteen months, she'll probably add some consonants, and by eighteen months, she'll have a vocabulary growth spurt of sorts, where you'll find her mumbling to herself like an old lady in the supermarket parking lot.

Before she hits her second birthday, she'll likely have two hundred words in her repertoire, having added up to ten new words *a day*—far more readily than you picked up French in high school. She'll even form some short sentences, like "Carry me" or "Juice, pwease." Soon, she'll even say three-word sentences until her third birthday, when it's likely she'll know upward of three hundred words, and not all of them having to do with cookies.

How do you know if your child has a speech delay? Consider these guidelines:

12–18 months: Your toddler says no words by fifteen months, or you can't understand a word she says by eighteen months.

18–24 months: Your toddler rarely speaks, doesn't say the consonants in words, and/or uses only single words, no "sentences."

2–3 years: Your toddler has trouble naming common everyday items, such as "ball" or "cat," doesn't use multiple-word phrases, and is hard to understand.

If this describes your toddler, consult your pediatrician to find out the next steps. Up to 10 percent of children have a developmental delay that can affect speech, but with intervention, they can improve. Note that some speech problems stem from hearing issues, so it might be wise to get your toddler's hearing screened.

Copycat. Copycat. Quit It! Quit It!

SPEAKING OF SPEAKING, you may find that your toddler starts to repeat what you say as she gets older. Sometimes it's fun and even cute when your toddler copies you. Oh, how the grandmas at the bagel shop love it when your toddler repeats to the salesclerk, "Poppy seed. Poppy seed." But it's not so cute when your toddler drops something on the ground and shouts, "Aw, crap!" now is it?

When your toddler is in this stage, be extra careful what you say, or else your neighbors might learn what you really think about their new "butt ugly, butt ugly, butt ugly" fence. But while your toddler's parroting might get old fast, don't discourage it. She's learning to sound out words and associate them with the correct items. Take heart: it's a phase that will pass— much sooner than your neighbor's grudge about what you think of her new fence, or her car, or her hair.

WE ASKED: Do you think it's easier or harder to have a toddler compared to a baby?

Easier: 33%
Harder: 17%
Not sure: 50%

First Steps: One Small Step for Your Toddler, One Giant Leap for You

I COULDN'T WAIT for my younger son, who hit twenty-five pounds before he reached his first birthday, to walk. He was getting too heavy to lug around. Besides, after a summer of watching him crawl face-first into our community lake, the upright position was very appealing: I was tired of bending over and scooping him up.

Walking is one of the most exciting milestones your toddler will reach, so keep your video camera fired up and ready. Also, keep the corners of your coffee table childproofed. You don't have to follow your toddler around with pillows in case she falls (heck, those diapers are pretty cushiony), but think of yourself as the Zamboni driver at a hockey game. You're trying to make the conditions as smooth as possible for the players.

Make sure that cords and other "tripables" are out of the way, and secure anything your toddler might grab to steady himself, such as tall floor lamps or wobbly shelves. Cover sharp corners on furniture or move them out of the room altogether. You can't put anything on the coffee table, anyhow, now that your toddler is mobile. (See Chapter 5 for more on toddler-proofing your home.)

Climb High: When Your Toddler Scales the Furniture and More

A LITTLE LESS fun is when your toddler figures out how to climb stairs, the kitchen table, the sectional, your mother's (formerly) white chair, and so on. Ugh! I remember spending one Easter following my toddler up the stairs and down the stairs and up the stairs and down the stairs and up the stairs. . . . It was like taking a step class in high heels. At least I burned off the chocolate Easter eggs I'd grabbed on the way to the stairs.

When my friend Helen had a toddler who liked to climb, she said it was like having another cat in the house. I guess he liked to be up high where he could keep an eye on his prey, or his mom. What can you do if you've got a climber?

First, know this stage is normal. Just because your brother's kid never once thought about climbing onto the kitchen counters and into the sink doesn't mean your toddler is out of control—or that you're to blame.

Next, just like the cat, give him something to climb. If you've got the room and the cash, invest in a toddler jungle gym, even if you have to buy a used one on Craigslist or eBay or at a second-hand shop. Think of it as his version of the kitty condo—better that than the couch.

Also, use some creative childproofing techniques. Lean the chairs against the kitchen table, so he can't climb on them. Or move them out of the kitchen altogether except at mealtimes. Attach bookshelves and the TV to the wall, so he doesn't pull them down on top of himself or the dog. And block the stairs the best you can. Climbers can usually scale a "childproof" gate, so you may have to lock him in the family room with you or barricade the stairs with something unclimbable. (For more details on childproofing, drop by Chapter 5.)

It worked for me!

"Never under any circumstance leave [toddlers] in another room alone while they are wide awake. If there is no way to get to that item on the very top shelf, I swear they will make a way."

—*Marlena, Augsburg, Tennessee*

Momma Said   **WE ASKED:** What surprised you the most about the toddler stage?

"How completely exhausting it is to stay calm after you've put the kitchen chair back for the fortieth time, so he can't climb up and get to the computer. He's doing it as I'm typing this . . . #41. I just put the kitchen chair back, a bit of screaming, and now he's dragging it again . . . #42. I guess I also didn't realize how determined these little creatures can be!"

—*Lisa, Blue Bell, Pennsylvania*

Drop, Giggle, Repeat:
When Your Toddler Plays Dropsies

THERE'S NOTHING LIKE a good game of "dropsies" to drive you absolutely bonkers. Your toddler, however, thinks it's the greatest activity ever created since ripping off his diaper and running naked through the house. He drops something, and you pick it up. Then he drops something, and you pick it up. Then he drops something. . . . wait a minute. Why pick it up? Because if you don't, he'll scream and melt into the ground like the Wicked Witch of the West at the end of *The Wizard of Oz*.

Toddlers love repetition. Whether they're repeatedly putting their toys into the toy box and then taking them out, or removing the refrigerator magnets and then putting them back on, and then removing them, they're having a blast. You? Not so much. Three readings of *My Big Truck Book* are quite enough for you, but your toddler just can't seem to get enough. And really, peekaboo was fun the first ten times, but after that, Mommy needs to reheat her coffee and go read the *New York Times* for a while no matter how many times little Ethan yells, "Again!"

Experts say that this stage of toddlerhood is all about learning cause and effect while exploring their worlds, yada, yada, yada. But it's also about reassurance for your toddler. Think about it: when you're one, everything is new. You might find comfort in the predictable—and your little one may find the predictable in throwing a toy out of the shopping cart a few dozen times.

Grin and bear it whenever you can, but don't feel guilty if you put the kibosh on repetitive activities after a while. Toddlers need to learn when a good thing turns bad, and frankly, sometimes you both need to put down *Green Eggs and Ham* and go to bed.

Okay, I admit it. . . .

"I used to be able to set him down as a baby, and he would still be there when I got back, usually sleeping. With a toddler, he is off like Dash from *The Incredibles*."

—*Michelle, Portland, Oregon*

Momma Said

WE ASKED: How did you maintain your sanity during some of the more trying days with your toddler?

"Prayer. And chocolate."

—*Shelley, Travis AFB, California*

Strike Three!
When Your Toddler Throws Stuff

I SHOULD HAVE known better than to turn my back on a toddler with a ball. Turns out, my nephew has really good aim. At just fourteen months, he was able to toss a sort of soft bouncy ball right at my head three times in a row. With each successful smack upside my head, he giggled and chased down the ball for more pitching practice. Turns out, nothing's more fun than hitting Aunt Jen in the head.

I know. I know. It's our own fault for encouraging him to throw the ball in the first place. But we had no idea what an arm that kid has, let alone such spectacular aim. Luckily, he threw a relatively soft object at me, because toddlers sometimes have difficulty differentiating between throwing a nice, soft ball and, say, Grandma's breakable tchotchkes that she's been collecting on eBay for the past five years. When your kid was a baby who threw, it was much cuter. But add the mobility and strength of a growing toddler, and ouch! Toddlers who throw can be downright dangerous. What can you do about it?

First, put away all your breakable, sentimental, and expensive goodies. Yes, you could spend your days teaching your toddler why she shouldn't chuck your Waterford wedding gifts across the room, but that could end up as your full-time job for the coming months. Save yourself the aggravation and put them away until she's older and better understands the difference between "throwable" and "designed to be thrown."

Second, give your toddler something to throw and a place to throw it, so he can get it out of his system. For instance, some kids love toy basketball nets. I gave one to my nephew for Christmas with the hopes that the net would be a more fun target than my head. Other toddlers don't have that kind of aim or patience, so a few supersoft balls and a room without breakable targets works best for them.

Finally, tie it down. I hooked various toys to some plastic chain links and attached them to my toddlers' car seats and strollers, so they could throw toys and retrieve them without Mommy's help (or my long sigh of aggravation and tedium).

Momma Said

WE ASKED: What's the worst piece of advice anybody ever gave you about teaching your toddler manners?

"'Leave the breakables out. They need to learn to not touch it.' Hello? Who wants to monitor Great-Grandma's precious candy dish 24/7? Inevitably, they will find the one minute you are not watching it to crash it to a million pieces. Can you not just put it away for a period of time, so you can bring it out later in one piece?"

—Sachia, Independence, Missouri

Jakers, It's a Shrieker!
Toddlers Who Can Pierce Your Eardrums

MY BEST FRIEND'S mom used to have a saying whenever we kids were too loud: "It goes right through me!" If you've got a shrieker, you know exactly what she meant. When your toddler is either happy or excited or ticked off, he shows it by letting out a long, loud, high-pitched noise that sounds like it could break glass or make your eardrums bleed if you got too close.

Conventional wisdom is that shrieking is all part of a toddler's exploratory nature. In other words, "Let's see what I can do with my voice!" But conventional wisdom never had to take a toddler to story time at the library, where the other mommies say things like, "What a set of lungs!" and "I don't think that my Amelia could make such a commanding noise." So what's a momma to do?

First, figure out what kind of shrieker you have, and adjust accordingly. Some kids might fit several profiles, so you may need a few different plans of attack.

The "Till Mommy Pays Attention" Shrieker

A toddler who shrieks to get your attention is a diabolical addition to your life. This is a kid who doesn't want to wait for you to finish your conversation with another grown-up, so she interrupts you with the kind of noise that sounds like it could take down low-flying planes by interfering with their radar.

Your biggest mistake is to stop talking and acknowledge it, because you're teaching her that shrieking works. Instead, make up a signal, such as a raised hand. She'll soon learn it means, "I hear you, but I'm not going to answer to shrieking." Then explain to the other grown-up what you're doing. It'll take a few agonizing times for your toddler to understand and to stop the madness, but it works if you're consistent and calm.

The "I'm as Happy as a Contestant on *Deal or No Deal*" Shrieker

This kid is tough to reprogram, because he's simply shrieking with the kind of joy grown-ups reserve for winning a new car on *Oprah*. He's happy, so he lets it rip. He might not even realize how loud he is. Or he does, and he just doesn't care.

You don't want to quash his one-kid party, but you can't let him shriek his way through the playground or Macy's or your brother's wedding. Now is the perfect time to teach him the value of using his "indoor voice" in lieu of shrieking like a cockatiel whose tail is being pulled. You'll often have to shush him and say in the nicest Mommy voice you can muster up, "Indoor voice, honey!" But eventually, he'll either get it or he'll pick up a new habit.

The "I'm Mad as Hell" Shrieker

She's mad as hell, and she's not going to take it anymore. At least, not without a migraine-inducing, everybody-stop-and-stare shriek heard 'round the world. She knows she's loud, and she knows you hate it. That's the whole point, silly. You take away the Barbie she just yanked off the shelves at Toys "R" Us, and she lets you know what she thinks of it—and you. Embarrassed by her outburst, you let her have the Barbie. Shrieking works for her, even if it's giving you ulcers.

But you have to stand firm, or else you're going to give her reason to keep on shrieking whenever she's angry. No matter how hard it is, don't let her know how much it rattles your insides. Take the Barbie away—or whatever made her angry in the first place—

and keep on going as though you are immune to her shrieks. It'll be embarrassing and bloodcurdling, but it's better than becoming the Mom of the Shrieker for the next year or so. Stick with your plan until she learns that shrieking doesn't work. You can add a time-out or some other short punishment to your repertoire, but don't yell, or you'll start a Battle of the Loudest, and we know who'll win that one. Just ask your ulcers.

Finally, stop your own shrieking. You know what I mean. You do it when you're home alone with your toddler and just can't take that god-awful noise of hers anymore. You let it loose until, soon, you sound just like her. She shrieks. You shriek. It's like the sound effects for *Saw II*. You may be *telling* her to stop shrieking, but you're *showing* her that Mommy shrieks, too. As much as it pains you to stay mum, Mom, you have to remain calm to get her to stop shrieking.

Toddling Toward Two

WHETHER YOU'RE HAPPY that Babyhood has come to a close, or you're mourning the loss of your cuddly bundle of obedience, you've got a toddler now, and life is changing—fast. But you might feel like it's changing too fast.

One minute your toddler is quietly "reading" a board book, and the next, she's high-jumping the "safety" gate so she can go dip her hands in the dog's water bowl. Remember, *this is normal*. A toddler who never toddles her way into trouble is as rare as a zebra in the woods of New Jersey.

When you have a toddler (or two or three) in the house, you may feel like you're trying to anticipate the behavior of a wild orangutan who has gotten hold of your garage door opener, your cell phone, and a box of Chex Mix. You just don't know what she'll do next. But take heart: other mothers are going through the very same thing you are right now, and many more have lived to talk about it. Find those mothers and share, share, that's fair, because your baby isn't a baby anymore.

Gimme a break

Change Your Mind-Set

If you think you need to spend every waking moment bettering your toddler's life, think again. Your toddler will do just fine for a few hours with a trusted relative, friend, or sitter while you go do something for yourself. Plus, you'll return more refreshed and ready to chase around a toddler again.

Just a minute!

Are You Ready for Toddlerhood?

Practice Test

Comprehension

Read the sample passage and answer the accompanying question.

Taryn the Toddler wants a Dora the Explorer cookie at the store, but her mother doesn't want her to have any sweets before dinner. Taryn throws a temper tantrum in the checkout aisle, while her mother pretends to be extremely interested in the store's credit card application.

In this passage, we learned that:

    a. Taryn could be heard from as far away as the Housewares aisle.
    b. Taryn really, really wants a Dora cookie.
    c. Taryn's mother really, really needs a vacation.
    d. All of the above.

Sentence Completion

Choose the phrase that best completes the sentence.
Stickers are a great:

    a. Potty-training reward.
    b. Way to get through the supermarket, even if I can't pry thirteen sticky Diegos from the shopping cart handle.
    c. Deal of difficulty to remove from clothing after they've been through the dryer.
    d. Furniture decorator, apparently.

Advanced Mathematics

Today, Lisa fed her triplets three chicken nuggets, five chicken nuggets, and six-and-a-half chicken nuggets, respectively. How many times did Lisa find chicken nuggets under the kitchen table?

a. 14½.

b. Feels like a million.

c. I don't know, but the dog is licking his chops.

d. Gotta go. They're all crawling out of their high chairs.

Chapter Two

Like Herding Cats:
Taking Your Toddler on the Go

 WE ASKED: What do you wish someone had told you about parenting toddlers before you had them?

"Buy running shoes."

—*Shelley, Travis AFB, California*

All the other mommies at music class had written their children's names neatly on name tags, which they placed on the front of their toddlers' shirts, right next to embroidered smiling Barneys or Elmos. Not me. I scribbled my boys' names and then slapped the name tags onto their backs as they ran out the door *again*. I figured that it would be the only way everyone else would learn my children's names, because my toddlers weren't about to sit in a circle and play the cymbals or the drums like all the other kids. No, they had places to go.

My boys got halfway down the hall before I caught up with them, hoisting them up by their overalls and lugging them back to music class, where we did it all over again. After two exhausting classes like that, we dropped out. If I wanted to spend forty-five minutes running and lifting, I'd have joined a gym. Besides, the other mommies were starting to talk about us. At least I think they were. I was in the hallway too often to know for sure.

Taking a toddler or two on the go can feel like herding cats: nobody's interested in going where you want them to go. Not when there's an orange ball in the bushes and ice cream in that store and look! A birdie!

While you might think of Lowe's as a nice place to buy a lamp or some paint for the bathroom, your toddler sees it as one huge playground with oh-so-fun aisles to race down and shelves right at eye level full of things to relocate or stuff into pockets. A toddler plus displays of fragile tiles equals a whole bunch of things you hadn't planned to purchase.

Taking a toddler on the go can feel like an excursion up Mount Everest, minus the helpful Sherpas and much needed rest along the way. But you can't just stay home until your kids start school. So how do you get out and about with toddlers in tow?

> "We go to Barnes & Noble, which has a Starbucks in it, and the kids play with the trains while I drink and read a book. That's one of my favorites!"
>
> —*Chrissy, Dillsburg, Pennsylvania*

It worked for me!

Packing for Chaos

No DOUBT YOU'VE already learned that the smallest people in the house require the most stuff, especially when you leave the house. Toddlers can actually need more stuff than babies, largely to replace what they lose, tear, spill, and otherwise ruin while on the go. The key is trying to foresee what they can possibly get into and then packing what you need to remedy the situation.

What to Pack for Short Trips

When you're getting ready to go out with your toddler, think of yourself as the officer in charge of provisions. If disaster strikes, you're the one everyone's going to blame when you don't have the right supplies to handle the situation. That doesn't mean that you have to pack up half the house just to go to the playground, but you should consider keeping certain things on hand, if nothing else, to make your life easier, including:

- **Extra wipes.** Not just for diaper cleanups, but for your toddler's hands. Personally, I don't think that hand sanitizers cut it for toddlers, who need more than just germ removal much of the time. Instead, I kept various-size containers of wipes, such as individually wrapped wipes, resealable packs, and big ol' tubs of wipes, in several locations, including in the diaper bag, my car, and my pockets.

- **Sippy cups, juice boxes, and refills.** My toddlers took a while to take a liking to juice boxes, so I packed up numerous sippy cups filled with their favorite drinks to take on the go. I packed milk in soft-sided coolers with ice packs. Juice came along unchilled, unless it was particularly hot outside. When they got older, I kept juice boxes in their diaper bag and, when the day wasn't boiling hot or below freezing, in my car.

- **Extra clothes.** I kept an extra outfit for my boys in the diaper bag and spare shirts and socks in my car, because I never knew when they'd pour a milk shake onto their laps or fall face-first into a puddle. In the winter, I brought along extra mittens and hats, which I bought cheap at the supermarket or at Kmart. In the summer, I always had extra swim diapers and sun hats, just in case.

- **Doubles.** When my sons went through their love affairs with various inanimate objects, including a toy moon, a tattered Scooby-Doo book, and toy trucks, I made sure I carried doubles of their favorites. That way, I didn't have to endure a long car ride home listening to their plaintiff wails for their long, lost (*insert name of lovey here*).

- **Potty-training gear.** I brought along toilet seat rings and reward stickers, so I could remain consistent with potty training while we were out. I also mapped out public toilets along our routes, just in case. Better to know where all the Burger Kings are along the way than to ruin a car seat. (Read more about potty training on the go in Chapter 4.)

> "We put a basket of toys on the backseat next to our toddler. Sometimes he (or I) exchanges one or two of the toys there for something that's kept in the house, so it's a 'rotating' collection. Just remember to clean the basket out every once in a while, or it'll get gross."
>
> —Susan, Edwardsville, Illinois

It worked for me!

> "My husband and I sang eighty choruses of 'I've Been Working on the Railroad' while driving through the Adirondacks with our twins. For some strange reason, that one song made them stop crying. Maybe it's the three different songs rolled into one. Maybe they were just too annoyed to cry while we sang. Who knows? All we know was that it worked."
>
> —Sharon, Port Orange, Florida

It worked for me!

What to Pack for Longer Trips

WHEN WE PACKED for our weeklong family annual vacation at the beach, we had to bring more clothes, toys, and equipment for our toddlers than we needed for ourselves. Sure, there were things we could have bought on the island, but for certain items, we were better off packing it up and hauling it along. Here's some of what you'll need:

- **Diapers.** If packing space isn't an issue, bring your toddler's diapers and training pants along, because it'll likely be cheaper to buy in bulk at your local warehouse store than at the convenience store near your vacation house or at the hotel gift shop. If you're traveling by plane, however, plan on buying when you get there, or you'll lose loads of valuable suitcase space.

- **Separates.** You're better off packing tops and bottoms than a bunch of jumpsuits for your toddler, because if he ruins his top when he dumps chocolate ice cream on it at the zoo, you only have to replace the shirt, not the entire outfit. Shirts and pants/skirts take up less room when you pack, too. Plus, separates are easier to get off if your toddler has to pee while you're on the go.

- **Anything that helps your toddler sleep.** If, for instance, you've gotten your toddler accustomed to falling asleep to the soothing emissions of a sound machine, for Pete's sake, pack it, or you probably won't get any sleep for the entire vacation. Same goes for pacifiers, blankies, stuffed animals, light-up mobiles, and favorite CDs, among other sleep aids.

- **A place to sleep.** I've seen some scary-looking cribs for rent while on vacation—contraptions that look like they've dropped in from the 1930s to trap your kid's fingers in them. If you're traveling by car, consider bringing along the portable playpen instead. If you're going by plane, have a backup plan, just in case the rent-a-crib is less than appealing. If you're visiting friends or family, ask if they've got a crib, playpen, or air mattress you can borrow. If you're stuck with a crib that doesn't look safe, put the crib's mattress on the floor near your bed and make sure you toddler-proof the room extra carefully. If your toddler is in a bed with rails, pack the bed rails if you've got the space. If not, prepare to move the vacation bed against the walls or the mattress to the floor.

- **Potty-training gear.** It might seem easier just to throw diapers back on your toddler for a week or two, but if you're in the process of potty training, this will confuse her and, therefore, set back your potty-training success. Bring whatever you're using to potty train while you're away from home. Or better yet, delay potty training altogether until after your vacation.

WE ASKED: What are the hardest parts of taking toddlers out and about with you?

Getting them ready to go: 52%
Getting them to stop dilly-dallying: 52%
Getting them into their car seats: 52%
Enduring temper tantrums: 52%
Keeping them from running off: 45%
Keeping them out of trouble: 41%
Lifting them to put them in the shopping cart, car seat, etc.: 33%
They want to be carried: 26%
They won't stay in the stroller: 22%
Keeping them entertained in the car: 19%
Trying to find a potty along the way: 15%
Losing things along the way: 11%

It worked for me!

"To do Christmas shopping, I felt no choice but to bring along the portable DVD player. He quietly watched *The Polar Express* while I shopped. The shoppers around me were sure thankful for the DVD player when it came time to stand in that long checkout line!"

—*Lynn, Belton, Missouri*

How to Get the Heck Out of the House

WHETHER YOU'VE GOT a haircut appointment and your babysitter didn't show, or you need to shop for dinner, sometimes you've just got to bring along your tot. Other times, your toddler is the guest of honor, like at the pediatrician's office or at a playgroup in the park, and has to go with you. How do you get out without freaking out?

Timing is everything. Do you really have to take your cranky toddler to the supermarket just before nap time, or can it wait until she's refreshed and, therefore, less likely to carry on like a celebrity who's been booted out of Spago? Think about it from your toddler's perspective: it's hard enough not having any say in what you do or where you go, but getting dragged to the furniture store at 9:00 PM on Friday night? Most grown-ups don't even want to do that.

Front-load the important stops. A toddler's mood can change fast, so you need to be prepared. Your sweet little one might run out of joy after stops at the bank, the pharmacy, and the post office, while you have yet to pick up the dry cleaning and an ice cream cake for tomorrow's birthday party at your house. Front-load the stops that can't wait until tomorrow.

Bring your bag of tricks. When you're on the road with your toddler, think of yourself as a magician on live television. Pack up anything you can use to entertain your toddler while you're stuck anywhere from the very boring and rather warm waiting area at your ob-gyn's office to a long line of traffic ten miles from home.

Shop online. When gas prices get high, it might be worth the price of shipping to order certain things online. My favorite things to buy online have long included Christmas gifts, books, makeup (reorders only—the colors look different on your computer screen), and clothes. Some grocery stores and pharmacies deliver, allowing you to keep your sick and cranky toddler at home while you get your shopping done online.

Add a happy stop. If your toddler knows that you always stop by the playground or his favorite ice cream shop after his visits to the pediatrician's office, your trip will go more smoothly. If he understands you won't take him there if he misbehaves elsewhere, it'll go even more swimmingly.

Bring a "wing-mom." A wing-mom is a friend who can help watch, entertain, or feed your toddler when you're on the go. Only you've got to promise to do the same for her kid. If you can bring along a wing-mom with older kids who can take care of themselves better than your toddler can, you'll get even better service. Better yet, bring Grandma. Wing-moms are most useful for long shopping trips, such as to outlet stores, or for trips to the water park, the zoo, or an amusement park.

"Bribery isn't always a bad thing."

—Crystal, San Antonio, Texas

It worked for me!

WE ASKED: What are the worst/most difficult places to take your toddler?

My doctor appointments: 41%
My hairstylist: 38%
The supermarket: 27%
Getting my toddler's hair cut: 21%
Target, the mall, other stores: 17%
Anywhere that's not toddler-proofed: 17%
Older siblings' activities: 14%
My in-law's house: 10%
The pediatrician's office: 10%
The car: 7%
The stroller: 3%
School: 3%
My parents' house: 0%

Other responses: church, nice restaurants, the post office, the library, airplanes, "anywhere that requires browsing on my part," and "inside when she wants to be outside."

> **It worked for me!**
>
> "My two-year-old will arch her back like a cat being put in water when she is being put into a shopping cart. I find that giving her a 'shopping list,' even if it's an old receipt, helps her settle down, because she feels like she's helping."
>
> —*Paula, Pittsburgh, Pennsylvania*

"Always bring snacks!"

—*Rebecca, Bluff City, Tennessee*

It worked for me!

"When our twins dilly-dallied, we counted *backward* from three. I'd warn, 'If you're not in that car within three seconds, I'm going to snatch you up by the ear and put you in it myself.' Then I held up three fingers and counted them down. '*Three. Two. One.*' Then (the hard part), if they didn't move, I had to pick up The Offender and do what I promised to do. They caught on pretty quickly. There's nothing like a major indignity to make them move a little faster next time."

—*Sharon, Port Orange, Florida*

It worked for me!

Troubleshooting on the Go

NOT EVERY TRIP out with your toddler will be an exhausting ordeal. I remember quite a few outings with my boys when I felt like I was in a Carter's commercial: the sun shone down on me and my happy kids in clean, well-fitting clothes as we shared Goldfish crackers and butterfly kisses at the park on a warm spring day. Then there were the other days when I felt more like I was the star of a made-for-TV movie where the mother ends up running away to live a secret life in the tropics with Rob Lowe.

What got me through those days? Troubleshooting. I became well versed in what can go terribly wrong when you're on the go with toddlers, and I learned how to anticipate and diffuse the most common situations, including:

- **The major meltdown.** The best way to deal with a tantrum-ing toddler is to get the heck out of wherever you are and don't look back. This sometimes means leaving a shopping cart full of stuff in the store (did that) or rushing out of a playdate (that, too). But it's the only way your toddler will learn that his manipulative superpowers have no effect on you. The worst thing you can do is threaten to leave and then not follow through. Your toddler will file this in his little brain for later when he'll have the meltdown of a lifetime where you least can stand it.

- **The rascal who runs off.** This one isn't just tiring, it's dangerous, too. If your toddler has a habit of dashing off in parking lots, down escalators, at street intersections, and so on, you need to keep her contained and restrained, no matter how much she hates it. Use your stroller's safety straps or buy one of those toddler leashes. Wal-Mart sells one that's designed to look like a cute monkey backpack. I've even seen safety alarms, not unlike the electronic ankle bracelets that prisoners under house arrest use, that sound when your toddler gets more than a few feet away. Finally, teach your toddler to stay close by rewarding good behavior and punishing her after she laughs maniacally while racing toward the automatic doors that lead to the road.

- **The "carry me" kid.** Your toddler can walk just fine, but he insists that you carry him everywhere, like Cleopatra through the common folk. But you've got enough to carry (and push and pull), thank you very much. Some kids like the better view, while others feel safer in your arms, especially if you're going somewhere new. Offer your hand instead, or promise to carry him "as far as that sign" or "until we get to the door." Sometimes, though, you're just going to have to carry him if you want to get anywhere fast.

- **The dilly-dallier.** You want to go now because her big brother's school bus is about to arrive, but your toddler wants to take a moment—or ten—to stop and check out the bug that's crawling in the garage. If you pick her up and run, she'll certainly scream, but you're going to have to. Don't spend the next few harrowing minutes explaining why "it's time to go now, honey," because she doesn't care. Tell her once, and if she doesn't take your hand, scoop her up. If you can build extra time for dilly-dallying before you go places, you'll both be happier. Just make sure she understands that she has limited time to stop and talk to the chipmunks.

- **The naked newbie.** If your toddler insists on stripping down to his skivvies, or refuses to wear socks (in the wintertime, no less), hats, coats, or even his car seat belts, you're not alone. This is a common issue among toddlers. I've heard of moms using safety pins to keep their toddlers' clothes on in public, but even safety pins can pop open (and hurt your child). Besides, if you're potty training, safety pins will make it all the more difficult. Instead, set up a "naked time," when your toddler can strip down to nothing—at home. And keep him away from the front door when the doorbell rings.

> **It worked for me!**
>
> "I prepared each boy when we'd go somewhere, and rarely did one act up. If one did, we left *immediately*, and said offending child went straight to his room, put on his jammies, and spent the rest of the night in the room, alone. We were big on 'bud nippin'."
>
> —*Carla, Omaha, Nebraska*

Gimme a break

Fill Your Tank

If the only time you get for yourself is during your commute to work, schedule some "me time." Splitting your time and energy between work and motherhood can be draining if you don't pencil in some time to recharge. Go out to lunch instead of eating at your desk or running errands. Make a monthly Sunday night movie date with girlfriends. Book yourself a Saturday morning massage every now and then. All these mom-centered activities will help you recharge, making you fresher for your kids and for work.

Just a Minute!

The 7 Habits of Highly Effective Toddlers

1. **Make loud noises in quiet places.** Don't want to be in that fancy restaurant where they don't let you color on the tablecloth? Just start singing "The Potty Song" Mommy taught you nice and loud, and before you know it, you'll be at McDonald's where you wanted to be in the first place.
2. **Chase the cat.** She knows all the best hiding places. Plus, she's got a fun stash of mouse-shaped toys behind the couch.
3. **Just say "No."** No, you don't want to put your snowsuit on. No, you don't want to eat green beans. No, you don't want to leave right now. If you say "no" often enough, you'll get what you want now and then—like Cheerios for dinner when Mommy says she's "had it." Whatever "it" is.
4. **Set up camp in Mommy and Daddy's bed.** It's a king-size bed, after all, and you're the king of the house.
5. **Kiss up to Grandma.** She's got candy in her purse, and she's willing to share it.
6. **Doze just enough to recharge your batteries.** Go ahead and nod off in the car on the way home from the supermarket. Then you won't need that nap Mommy keeps talking up, and you can go back to chasing the cat. And keep going . . . and going . . . and going.
7. **Treat the potty like a foreign country.** It's a place you'd like to visit someday, sure, but not until it fits into your plans.

Chapter Three

If You'll Just Go to Sleep, I'll Take You to Disney World in the Morning: Sleep Issues

They finally fell asleep. Both of my toddlers, one under the weather and the other just plain fussy, had been fighting sleep all night, until both of them fell asleep—in my bed, right where I sleep next to my husband, who was also catching z's.

I thought about sneaking down the hall to sleep in my son's bed but worried what would happen if a kid woke up and found me missing. Certainly, he'd shout for me, thereby waking up his brother, and then they'd both cry while my husband desperately tried to calm them until the Mommy Valium showed up. So I curled up at the foot of the bed like a cat. Also like an idiot.

My mother never would have tried to doze off at her children's feet like a bichon frise who had just given birth. So where did I get this idea that I needed to be at the ready for my toddlers' every waking need? From several hundred consecutive nights of interrupted sleep, that's where. I was so tired that it was clouding my judgment.

But it really started when the nurses at the neonatal intensive care unit who had taken care of my first baby, who was premature, advised me to care for him "on demand," even though they had, in fact, fed him on a comparably cushy schedule of every three hours. And it all went downhill from there. As a result, I wound up trying just about every so-called "sleep solution" I could find until my younger son finally, blessedly, slept through the night— at sixteen months old.

I'll share what worked and what didn't when it came to getting my toddlers to sleep through the night and to nap during the day. If you feel like the only mother who has ever promised her toddler a trip to Disney World in exchange for a snooze, so Mommy can get a break, don't. I've been there, done that.

How Much Sleep Does Your Toddler Need?

Age	Daytime Sleep	Nighttime Sleep	Total
12 months	2–2½ hours in two naps	11–11½ hours	13–14 hours
18 months	2 hours in one nap	11–11½ hours	13–13½ hours
2 years	1–2 hours in one nap	11 hours	12–13 hours
3 years	1–1½ hours in one nap	10½–11 hours	11½–12½ hours

WE ASKED: Does/did your toddler sleep through the night?

Yes, pretty much every night: 71%
Sometimes: 14%
Rarely: 14%

Bedtime Battles

THE ONE THING I somehow got right about getting my kids to sleep at night was bedtime. I rarely had the bedtime battles that other parents went through, like the toddler I know who wouldn't go to bed at night without first being rocked to sleep and the toddler who stayed up past eleven every night until she passed out from exhaustion.

But my younger son did go through a period where he refused to get into his bed. What worked? Sticking to a bedtime routine and not caving in when he stood outside my door at night, sobbing as though I'd just given his puppy away to Ozzy Osbourne or something equally dastardly.

Routine, Routine, Routine

IF YOU SET UP—and stick to—a regular bedtime routine, you'll help signal to your toddler that it's nearing the time to go to bed. (Staying there is another issue, but I'll get to that later.) The younger your child is when you start, the better, but it's never too late to get into a good bedtime routine.

There are two main keys to the bedtime ritual: consistency and relative peace. Bedtime isn't the best time to jam out to your Raffi CDs, because it probably won't tire out your toddler. Rather, you'll just wind her up like the Energizer Bunny. She may not necessarily need total silence to get to sleep, but you can help signal that it's time for bed by slowing down the activity a bit.

WE ASKED: What was the worst part about having a toddler?

"The lack of sleep and the need for constant energy."

—*Beth, Warrington, Pennsylvania*

Bedtime Dos and Don'ts

Do START A **bedtime routine.** Spending hours in an elaborate bedtime ceremony not unlike a five-day Indian wedding is both exhausting and unnecessary. All you really need is about a half hour and a plan. Our bedtime ritual included bath time, teeth brushing, a few inane books about trucks, and a quick snuggle. And, except for the month my younger son decided instead to cry until he passed out on our hardwood floor, that plan worked.

Do adjust your bedtime ritual to your toddler's personality. Some toddlers find the bath as exhilarating as a brisk swim in a mountain lake at dusk, so you might want to save it for the morning. Others don't have the patience to sit for a nightly reading of *Goodnight Moon*, so the bedtime book might have to wait until they're older and can sit longer than a few sentences and some gentle pleading.

Do be the boss. I found that it's better when your toddler doesn't have too much say in the bedtime ritual, or else you'll find yourself frantically pacing the room like a husband in a 1960s maternity ward waiting area while your toddler agonizes over which pj's to wear or which stuffed animal gets the honor of sleeping in his bed tonight. If you've got a mini–control freak for a kid, however, you might have to cede some of the decision making just to keep peace. Just keep it to a minimum, or else you'll probably doze off while he takes his nightly power trip.

Don't rock your toddler to sleep. If you do it so often that it becomes part of the bedtime ritual, your toddler will have a hard time falling asleep—or falling back to sleep—without your help. If you're already rocking your toddler to sleep, start weaning her off of it as soon as possible. The older she gets, the stronger her resistance builds, and the harder it is to break the habit. And who has the strength to rock a sixty-pound kid to sleep?

Don't rush to check on your toddler every time he makes a noise *unless he seems scared or sick.* Some kids need to play quietly or to talk to themselves before they go to sleep. Others like to talk into the baby monitor like they're ordering a Big Mac and fries at the drive-through. If you rush to see what he wants every time he summons you, you'll spend his toddler years being treated like room service on the high rollers' floor at a Vegas hotel. If he's scared, however, you need to reassure him that you'll be there when he needs you. And if he's sick, put aside your bedtime routine until he feels better.

Don't bribe or threaten, no matter how tired you are. I admit that I once promised to drive my son to the Crayola Factory—ninety minutes away—if he'd just forget about the green crayon he'd lost and go to sleep. Instead, he shouted for his crayon even louder, waking up his little brother. As a result, we all wound up awake—until 4:00 AM. Bribes and threats reveal to your toddler just how desperate you are, thereby making it even more fun to stay awake and watch Mommy implode. I know. I've been there.

A Word About Grooming

AS YOUR TODDLER becomes more independent, it's a great time to teach her about grooming. Put a little shampoo on her hand and let her wash her own hair before you finish up the job. (In other words, wash more than her bangs and her rubber ducky, like she did.) Teach her how to wash herself with soap and how to dry off with a towel. Let her comb her hair (as long as there are no knots). Good grooming now makes it easier to introduce potty training later, when you'll be singing about washing hands. You'll see.

Your toddler is still too little to brush her own teeth. In fact, dentists recommend that you brush your child's teeth until she's at least six years old. Use a soft-bristled brush, preferably one with a favorite cartoon character on the handle so that your toddler looks forward to brushing. Put a tiny bit of fluoride toothpaste in tasty kids' flavors (mmm, bubblegum) on the toothbrush, and brush all the sides of her teeth that you can reach. Of course, try to make sure she doesn't swallow the toothpaste.

Note that most dentists recommend a first dental visit at age two, so ask around to see where your neighbors take their kids. Dentists who specialize in pediatrics will know how to make your toddler comfortable.

For Cryin' Out Loud

WHEN MY YOUNGER son was sixteen months old and still waking me up at night, my mother complained, "Well, *you* didn't sleep through the night until you were four months old."

Amateur.

After years of chronic sleep deprivation, I was exhausted, frustrated, and desperate. In fact, when I received a letter from a local sleep study clinic, I behaved as though I'd just won the $64 million PowerBall. "They want me for a sleep study!" I sang, before I even opened it.

It was the only way I thought I could get a full night's sleep, because all the other methods I'd tried, including co-sleeping (aka full-contact kickboxing), loving persuasion (read: Mommy is a pushover), and playing with toy cars at three o'clock in the morning didn't work. Unfortunately for me, however, the owner of the sleep clinic was a neighbor inviting me to a block party. *Maybe I could nap in the bouncy castle when no one's looking*, I thought.

So, after some 850 consecutive nights of interrupted sleep, I did the unthinkable: I let my toddler cry it out—*for four hours*—after he woke up in the middle of the night, while my husband pleaded, "Shouldn't we just go pick him up?" But I kept repeating the mantra my mother-in-law had given me: "There was nothing wrong with him all day, and there's nothing wrong with him now."

It was indeed one of the toughest nights of my life as a mother, but here's the thing: it worked. After that harrowing, horrible night, my toddler—and, *finally*, I—slept through the night pretty much every night thereafter. With regular sleep, we were both happier, and I stopped drooling outside the front window of mattress stores.

I wasn't alone. One-third of kids under age five have "disturbed nighttime sleep," which, I suppose, is a euphemism for "No sleep for the grown-ups." Even more refuse to nap even when they need to. If you've got one or more of those kids, understand that you're not alone, either, no matter what your mother tells you. There are all sorts of books, DVDs, and websites designed to help you help your toddler sleep through the night. Find the one that's right for you, and you, too, can sleep all night long—without signing up for a sleep study.

WE ASKED: Does your toddler sleep through the night?

"My older child never did, and my youngest does almost every night!"

—*Angie, Indianapolis, Indiana*

WE ASKED: What kinds of things have you done to get your toddler to sleep at night?

Sticking to a routine: 63%
Let him/her sleep in my bed: 56%
Drink a sippy cup or bottle: 38%
Play music: 31%
Read books: 31%
Threats: 25%
Watch TV: 19%
Use a pacifier: 13%
Bribery: 13%
Drive him/her around in the car: 13%
Nothing. I just put him/her in the crib/bed: 13%

Is It Time for the Big-Kid Bed?

FOR OUR FIRST son, the decision to move out of his crib and into a bed was easy: we needed the crib for the baby. A few months before he became a big brother, we moved his crib into the nursery, telling him that only babies sleep in cribs. Besides, he was already climbing out of his crib. Better to give him a shorter drop to the ground before he landed himself in the E.R.

He adjusted surprisingly well for a seventeen-month-old. Somehow, he didn't put it together that if he could climb out of his crib, he could also hike himself over his bed rails. Perhaps we just got lucky, because I've heard horror stories from other parents who spent night after night returning their toddlers to their beds. What should you know about transitioning your toddler from crib to big-kid bed? Here's the scoop.

When Do I Make the Switch?

- **Find the right age *for your kid*.** Most toddlers make the switch from crib to bed between eighteen months and two and a half years, but please don't make this another milestone competition. Your kid will be ready when your kid is ready—preferably before she gets too big for the crib. If she's climbing out of her crib, it's time.

- **Tall kids transition earlier.** The taller your toddler, the sooner you should make the switch. If your toddler's crib rails hit him at chest level or lower when he's standing in his crib, it'll be easier for him to get out—or fall out. (Adding a NERF basketball hoop to teach him to dunk along the way is optional.)

- **Avoid making changes during stressful times.** Like any other major transition, don't make the switch from crib to bed during a particularly stressful time, such as when you've just added a baby to the family or during a move or a divorce. That's why we switched our older son *before* the baby arrived, and part of why it worked.

How Do I Get My Toddler from the Crib to the Bed?

- **Make it fun.** I told my kids that "big boys get big-boy beds." I didn't drag them along to pick out a twin bed. Even I hate going mattress shopping (unless the salesclerks will watch my kids while I nap, of course). But I did bring my toddlers along to pick out their new big-boy sheets and bedding. Bye-bye, Pooh. Hello, planes!

- **Skip the toddler bed.** It really isn't necessary to go out and buy a toddler bed when a regular bed will do. All it means is more money and yet another transition to make later on. Of course, if Daddy wants to build a fire truck bed frame for his little boy, it'll be easier to size it to a toddler bed. And it'll keep them both busy for a few Saturdays.

- **Childproof.** We added bed rails to my toddlers' big-boy beds so they wouldn't roll over and fall out of bed in the middle of the night. If you've got an escape artist on your hands, you might want to add a safety gate in her doorway. If she can scale that faster than a perp on a fence on *Cops*, shut her door and add a childproof doorknob. Or you can give her small rewards for staying in her bed at night.

"We co-sleep, so at bedtime we all go to the bedroom. **It worked for me!** My son plays with us for a few minutes and then lays down and goes to sleep on his own. The actual act of going to the family bed has been routine enough to create the habit of sleeping there for him."

—Gretchen, Winder, Georgia

WE ASKED: Does your toddler nap?

Yes, just about every day: 71%
Sometimes: 29%
Never: 0%

How long does your toddler usually nap?

He/she never naps: 0%
Half an hour or less: 6%
One hour or less: 12%
1–2 hours: 35%
2–3 hours: 47%
More than 3 hours: 0%

Nap Time: Better Than Chocolate

I used to get angry when the phone rang during nap time. Didn't everyone know this was the only time during the day I had a moment to myself . . . to watch reruns of *The Daily Show* before falling into a deep, drooling sleep on the couch? If I managed to get my kids to nap at the same time, I felt as though I had made an elaborate beach sculpture of Washington, D.C., for the Guinness Book of World Records. *Nobody move! You'll ruin it!*

When my kids didn't sleep well at night, nap time was nothing short of the restoration of my sanity. Luckily, my older son was a star napper; he slept upward of three hours just about every day until he turned four years old. His little brother could nap up to two and a half hours at a clip, depending on how exhausted he was from keeping me up all night. The trick was to get them to nap at the same time. Also, to muffle the phone and the cat.

Most afternoons, I managed to get them to fall asleep around the same time with little fanfare, bribery, or threats. But some days, I resorted to driving them around the neighborhood until they finally fell asleep and I memorized the numbers on my neighbors' mailboxes. Other days, I gave up and started counting the hours until bedtime.

You're not the only one who needs your toddler to nap. Your toddler does, too, usually until he's three, though some stop earlier, like my younger son who quit, much to my chagrin, a few days after his big brother did. Experts say that toddlers need their naps to restore their energy after all those developmental milestones they reach, not to mention all those mornings playing with your wooden spoons and Tupperware like a one-man band in *The Little Rascals.*

Experts also say it's a chance for your toddler to learn to self-soothe or entertain himself to sleep, though mine didn't seem to remember that lesson at 2:00 AM, or 4:00 AM, or 5:15. Whatever the reason, you know when your toddler needs a nap, but getting one in every day can require a little orchestration.

WE ASKED: How did you maintain your sanity during some of the more trying days with your toddler?

"Making sure he had a nap every day.
The days he refused would kill me."

—*Kelly, Wickliffe, Ohio*

How to Do Nap Time

Some of the same rules that apply at bedtime work for nap time, while others are just for daytime hours. Here's what you should know.

Stick to a schedule. Try to make nap time close to the same time every day, even if that means hightailing it out of the gym just when you've finally figured out how to use the elliptical machine without falling off, or telling Grandma she's got to let her grandchild lie down for an hour or two no matter how much she wants to spoil him some more. If your toddler is in day care during the week, you've got a head start, because chances are they've got a set nap routine that you can follow at home. If not, make your own routine and stick to it as much as possible.

Keep it quiet. It can be hard for a toddler to lie down for a nap when there's a lot going on in the home. Try to keep older children and pets quiet at nap time. You might even want to use a sound machine that drowns out noises, though I'd avoid one that uses water noises, especially when you're trying to potty train. Pull down the shades, give your toddler her favorite love object (that isn't you), and then get out of the room.

Keep it simple. Don't make the nap time ritual as elaborate as bedtime, or you'll be scrambling to read a book, sing a lullaby, yada, yada, yada, in the middle of the day when you're likely the most crazed. The simpler your nap time ritual, the more likely your toddler will nap in the playpen at your sister's house while you two catch up on life beyond the nursery.

Be flexible. I know it sounds contradictory when I just told you to stick to a schedule, but there are days when you'll have no choice but to improvise nap time, including: when your toddler is sick, when you're on the go and can't get home, when there's construction or other loud noises going on outside her window, when your older kids have an activity during nap time, or when you're sick and really, really need your toddler to nap so you can rest your head right now and not an hour from now, *pleeeeeease God.*

Don't ruin bedtime. Don't let your toddler's nap time usurp the power of bedtime by starting it too late or letting it last too long. Managing your toddler's sleep is part art, part science.

One Nap or Two?

Some moms transition their toddlers to one midday nap around their first birthdays. Others wait until they're closer to eighteen months or even two years old. Who's right? It all depends on your kid—and your schedule.

My younger son used to be an early riser. He even woke me up at 5:30 AM now and then to tell me he was tired. (Yeah? I'll show you tired, kid.) As a result, he needed to keep his morning nap a little longer than his big brother did, a month or so beyond his first birthday. You know, because it's tiring waking Mommy up in total darkness every morning.

But I needed my sanity, also known as "two toddlers sleeping at once," so I started pushing his morning nap later and later until he had one afternoon nap that coincided with at least part of his big brother's daily marathon siestas. Did he start sleeping later each morning? Nope. But he adjusted to his one-nap-a-day schedule by sleeping longer at nap time. Can I get an Amen?

Choosing when to merge your toddler's nap into one is a personal decision based on your toddler's needs *and yours*. While your oldest child may have had a sleep environment suitable for royalty visiting the White House, your youngest might start nap time in the car on the way home from her big sister's preschool every weekday afternoon. And guess what? You're not the only mom winging it at nap time. Just do what you've got to do, and everyone will turn out fine in the end.

WE ASKED: What was the best part about having a toddler?

"Having everyone say, 'You have a toddler?' and me not bursting into tears."

—*Susan, Montville, New Jersey*

WE ASKED: What do you wish someone had told you about parenting toddlers before you had them?

"How important it is to take breaks from child care."

—*Julie, West Chester, Pennsylvania*

Gimme a break

Get Out with the Girls

Set up a regular get-together once a month or so to get out with your girlfriends—and I don't mean meeting with full strollers at Baby Gap. Remember, you're not just a mommy, but a woman, too—a woman who would probably love to see a movie that's not animated with talking elephants for a change.

 Just a Minute!

Goodnight, Soon?

In the great Barney room

There was a Tickle Me Elmo

And a loud cartoon

And a picture of—

Eeyore napping at noon.

And there were three little Teletubbies sitting on chairs.

And two rolled-up socks

And a pair of blocks

And a little toy cell phone

And pj's from Go, Diego, Go!

And a comb and a brush and a toddler in a rush

And a tired mom whispering hush.

Goodnight soon?

Goodnight toons.

Goodnight Eeyore napping at noon.

Goodnight Elmo and this mess of a room.

Goodnight socks.

Goodnight blocks.

Goodnight Diego

And goodnight . . . where'd you go?

Goodnight to the potty.

Goodnight, though your sleep is spotty.

Goodnight brush . . . goodnight, now flush!

And goodnight to the mom whispering hush.

Goodnight Baby Bop.

Goodnight there.

Goodnight toddlers everywhere.

Chapter Four

The Most Labor-Intensive Milestone: Potty Training Your Toddler

"Relax a bit. Remember, no one will ever say, 'Introducing the Homecoming Queen, who didn't pee on the potty until she was over three and a half!' or 'Congratulations to Johnny, who graduated from college with honors, and pooped in his pants until he was four.'"

It worked for me!

—Anne, West Milford, New Jersey

I just wanted to take my kids to the shoe store, but I might as well have been planning to take them cross-country— on foot. My son was in the middle of potty training, and I didn't want to set him back by taking him out for new light-up sneakers, even though he'd peed on the last pair.

So I called the shoe store and asked if we could use their bathroom when we got there. "Lady," the salesclerk said, "nobody has asked me that in twenty years." When I explained I was in the middle of potty training, he acquiesced. Turns out, he had potty trained two boys himself, so he understood. And we did, indeed, use his bathroom.

Mom, 1. Toddler-size bladder, 0.

My two boys potty trained differently from each other. One son sat on a kid-size potty in the middle of the kitchen while watching "It's Potty Time!" on video. (I've *still* got one of its grating songs stuck in my head: "I use my potty when I have to poop." Blah!) The other son went straight to the toilet—but, sadly, didn't skip the video.

One child learned to use the potty when it was summertime, supposedly among the most ideal times to train because it's easier to peel off a pair of shorts than, say, overalls, a snowsuit, hat, gloves, boots, and a hood full of snow mixed with gravel and, probably, Cheerios. Yet, my other kid potty trained a few weeks before Christmas. (Thank you, Santa!) We just didn't go anywhere for ten days, except, of course, to the shoe store.

By the time I was done with the training pants, rewards, potty videos, and "Uh-ohs!" on the dining room rug, I had learned a valuable lesson: whatever your mother and mother-in-law tell you about how they potty trained their kids is a big, fat lie. Or at least it's a fuzzy memory made even fuzzier by a few long decades and a whole different style of parenting that doesn't suit today's moms. Potty training today is different than it was a generation ago. How will you handle it?

"Your grandma did not have your mom potty trained at nine months. C'mon, really think about it: could they even get to the toilet?"

—*Sachia, Independence, Missouri*

Are You Ready to Stumble?

CONTRARY TO POPULAR belief, a sign of potty training readiness is *not* when your mother says it's time to start. "Readiness" actually means that your *toddler* is ready to potty train, though don't expect that to mean he'll necessarily ditch his diapers by dinnertime.

Potty training is a process that takes some kids longer than others. And if it's your kid that's taking his sweet time, it can feel painfully long. And wet. Like your carpet. But I can help you shorten the learning curve while making you feel less alone along the road to underpants.

I learned that no two kids train exactly the same when my younger son showed signs of readiness much earlier than his big brother did. Only it turned out he was just having fun imitating his three-year-old brother. As a result, we spent a good two months getting him to pee in the potty "just like a big boy," only to discover that the whole thing was nothing more than a novelty to him.

When I finally caught on that he was no more ready to potty train that I was to follow him around the house, singing, "I use my potty when I have to pee," so soon after having trained his big brother, I put the whole thing on hold until he was truly ready—

a whole year later. In the end, potty training probably took him less time overall than if I'd stuck to it when he started copying his big brother way before he was truly ready for the potty.

> "I knew it was time to potty train when she understood what 'No peein', no poopin'' meant when I put her in panties in the afternoon."
>
> —Chrissy, Dillsburg, Pennsylvania

It worked for me!

"But Other Toddlers Have Potty Trained Faster/Sooner Than Mine!"

I remember feeling guilty that my son's friend in his tot play class had started walking sooner than he did. (I admit it: I wanted to trip him the first time I witnessed his successful stumble from the slide to the play tunnel.) But every kid reaches milestones, including potty training, at his own pace. My son is well beyond his toddler years, and yes, he can walk just fine. He's also potty trained, even though some of his friends ditched their diapers sooner than he did. Trust me: in another year or so, no one will remember who trained when.

"I Admit It: I Throw Diapers on My Kid When It's Just Plain Easier for Me."

We all have those days when the kids are hanging off our belt loops, whining; the cat is using the new couch as a scratching post;

the groceries spill out of the bag and down the hill into a ditch; and the power goes out while you're uploading three hundred vacation photos online. On those days, you get a "cheat," just like the folks on *Are You Smarter Than a Fifth Grader*. Just don't cheat so much that you end up failing in the end. See page 65 about the downsides of switching back and forth to diapers.

Fifteen *Real* Signs of Readiness

Many kids start potty training when they're two, but don't assume that your toddler's second birthday is a sign of readiness. Below are some of the major signs of readiness, but keep in mind that your toddler doesn't have to meet *all* of them to be ready to potty train. If she's reached at least three of them, you might want to give potty training a try.

1. **Stays dry for up to two hours and through a nap.** If your toddler woke up dry only after a twenty-minute catnap in the car two weeks ago Tuesday, he's probably not ready for the potty. But if he routinely stays dry for at least two hours, it may be time to introduce the potty to him.

2. **Can follow instructions.** If your toddler is the type of kid who will listen to your request to, say, put her shoes in the closet or put her sippy cup in the sink *and* actually does it much of the time, she'll be more likely to follow your instructions for potty training, too.

3. **Cooperates.** Does your toddler just say "no" nowadays? If he's more likely to continue finger painting the guinea pig

until you have to pick him up and move him away from poor Fluffernutter, you might want to wait until he's in a more agreeable state to start potty training.

4. **Can sit down for minutes at a time.** A restless toddler won't sit on the potty for very long, leaving you to measure your potty training sessions in seconds, rather than minutes. If you're frantically trying to distract your toddler to get her to sit on the potty like a novice dog trainer trying to teach pit bulls not to chase the cat that just sauntered by, it's most likely too soon to introduce her to the potty.

5. **Has bowel movements at about the same time every day.** If, for instance, he's pooping right after *Barney & Friends* ends each morning, it's a safe bet that you'll eventually be able to get him to poop on the potty around that time.

6. **Shows you she's gotta go potty.** If she hides in the dining room every time she poops, or says, "Uh-oh!" while she's peeing, it means she's aware that she needs to go to the potty, even if you have to lead her there.

7. **Can say "pee" and "poop."** It makes it a whole lot easier to understand that your toddler is about to pee in the middle of Wal-Mart when he can tell you he's gotta go.

8. **Tells you before she pees or poops.** Lucky you if your toddler actually tells you she's about to pee. Don't worry if she makes it to the potty or not. In time, you can teach her to let you know *before* the flood gates open.

9. **Asks to use the potty.** Then you don't have to wonder if every pause, grimace, or trip behind the toy box means it's time to rush to the bathroom. He actually *wants* to use the potty and tells you about it. It's like winning the potty training lottery!

10. **Is uncomfortable in dirty diapers.** The child who doesn't mind sitting in poop until your visitor asks, "What's that smell?" is less likely to tell you when she needs the potty. You might want to wait a few more weeks or months to start potty training.

11. **Can take off his diaper and undress himself.** If you've got one of those toddlers who likes to strip down and answer the front door naked, he can probably get everything off for the toilet, too. Even a kid who'll pull down his pants now and then can do it in the bathroom, too.

> **Okay, I admit it. . . .**
>
> "I tried candy, tried yelling, and I'm convinced that boys do not fully connect the brain to the bottom until they're three years and three months old."
>
> —*Susan, Montville, New Jersey*

12. **Asks for training pants or underpants.** If she wants to be a "big girl," well then, hurray! Those Disney princesses (or cars, or whatever) sure do motivate a toddler to potty train.

13. **Shows interest in the potty.** I don't mean that he likes to float his toy boat in the toilet or flush your spare change.

I mean that he finds the potty and all its related functions interesting and fun.

14. **Is proud when she does something good.** It'll make it easier for rewards and praise to work in your bag of potty training tricks.

15. **Likes to make you happy.** And if Momma's happy, everybody's happy.

Momma Said

The Real Poop on Potty Training:

Thirty-three percent of MommaSaid moms started potty training when their older children were between 25 and 30 months old. For their younger children, however, nearly 40 percent waited until their kids were between 31 and 36 months old.

Let's Get This Potty Started

SO YOUR TODDLER is ready to potty train. Now what? Before you put her on the potty, gear up. Minimally, you'll need a toilet and a toddler. But there's a whole industry of potty training stuff out there designed to help you through the process. Does your toddler really need the Royal Potty Chair, a plastic potty seat that plays songs befitting a king or queen that promises "royal fanfare with each success!" I dunno. But I do know I'd like the same thing whenever I sit at the dinner table.

WE ASKED: What do we need to potty train?

Underpants: 80%
Kid-size potty for home: 67%
Training pants: 60%
Potty training books for my child: 53%
Potty seat to place over toilet at home: 53%
Portable wipes: 33%
Portable potty seat or potty: 27%
Potty training books for me: 27%

Potty Versus Toilet Ring

SO DO YOU go out and buy a kid-size potty, or do you buy a ring to place on your toilet? We started with a potty simply because someone had given us one as a baby gift. We were new parents, so what the heck did we know? We figured that the friends who had picked it out for us had potty trained their two daughters, so they must be sure of what we'd need.

But the splash guard on the potty was designed a little too close for my son. As a result, when he peed, it poured—sometimes straight up in the air. We cleaned it and gave it away, choosing instead to buy a different potty that was better suited to his, uh, parts.

Frankly, though, I grew tired of playing sanitation worker, cleaning up the results of his potty successes. You can shout "Hurray for you!" all you want, but when you're carrying a plastic cup full of pee and poop across the kitchen floor, it's hard to remain enthusiastic for long. Eventually, we put the seat from the potty right onto the toilet and that worked for him just fine. But for my younger son, we skipped the potty altogether and went straight to the ring for the toilet.

When we were potty training, I kept one toilet ring in our powder room and one in my boys' bathroom. I also kept one at each grandmother's house, and I brought one along whenever we went out, just in case. I just stuffed it into a plastic bag and carried it along with our diaper bag.

I know it sounds cumbersome to lug around a big padded toilet ring with smiling Big Birds and Ernies on it, but it was necessary after the horrible Pinching Incident. That's when we tried a portable folding potty ring, a plastic seat cover your toddler can use on the go, especially on those awful public toilets that are either filthy or just plain scary-big.

Only, when my toddler sat on it, his butt got pinched by the darn thing, and he screamed. I thought for sure he'd never want to sit on the toilet again until well into adulthood, but I managed to save the day, or at least years of therapy, by promising him that he'd never see the "bad potty ring" ever again.

Stores still sell plastic folding potty covers, and I read one online review in which a mother complained that hers pinched her kid's behind, too, so be careful if you buy one. One mother complained that her portable seat, featuring a favorite cartoon character, didn't fit some oversized public toilets. As a result, her daughter's leg got caught between the little cover and the big toilet seat. As Dora would say, *Aye carumba!*

> "Have a potty chair on every level, so that a beginner can get to it in time."
>
> —*Carla, Omaha, Nebraska*

It worked for me!

M&M'S: Reward or Bribery?

MOST TODDLERS LOVE praise and rewards for doing something well. Then again, don't we all? But when does a reward become bribery? When you promise your little tyke breakfast with Cinderella at Disney World if she poops on the potty, perhaps.

I have found that rewards for potty training work well if you keep them rooted in reality. Whenever my kids had success on the potty, I put stickers on their shirts. On a good day, they'd have a chest full of stickers, like five-star generals, by the time Daddy got home from work. Then he'd shower them with praise, and the whole thing felt like one big happy public service announcement for positive parenting.

Of course, I found out the hard way what happens when you forget to remove stickers from clothing before they hit the clothes dryer. I believe this is how iron-on T-shirt transfers were invented, except in our case, Thomas the Tank Engine's smiling face usually melted off, leaving behind a white sticky mess on the boys' overalls, and their sweatshirts, and the nice sweaters Grandma gave them.

Some parents use candy as rewards, while others believe this only promotes sugary excess, if not childhood obesity. I think a few Skittles never hurt anyone, but I didn't use them as rewards because I knew I'd eat them in lieu of lunch. Other moms use progress charts, toys, dinner out, books, videos, and cold, hard cash, which works great if you've got a junior Donald Trump in your house.

> "We did a potty penny jar for my daughter. Five pennies for number one and fifteen pennies for number two. She loved to shake it after going potty!"
>
> —*Karyn, Northville, Michigan*

It worked for me!

WE ASKED: What kind of rewards did you dole out for potty training?

- Calling Grandma
- Cheering, clapping, and praising
- Stickers
- Special big kid underpants
- Toys
- Candy
- A special dinner at the end of the week

> "We got an M&M'S dispenser. They got one push for going number one and two pushes for going number two in the potty."
>
> —*Deb, Montgomery, Alabama*

It worked for me!

The Potty Training Challenge

POTTY TRAINING IS like a hike in the woods. It could turn out to be short and easy, or it would wind up a long, harrowing trip where you often feel lost and wish someone could come rescue you. If you're one of the lucky ones who get to the end of the trail without breaking a sweat, congratulations! But the rest of us need stamina and, perhaps, a field guide. Here's what else you need to bring along on your potty training challenge:

- **Persistence.** On those really exhausting days, it's tempting to throw diapers on your toddler and go out without needing to map out every public bathroom between your house and Baby Gap. But a study by the Medical College of Wisconsin found that switching back and forth to diapers confuses kids and slows the potty training process. Once you start, keep at it as much as you can stand it.

- **Consistency.** Maybe your mom is doing you a favor by watching your kids while you go get a haircut without a toddler playing in the hair clippings under your feet. But that doesn't mean that potty training should pause while you're out. Everyone who takes care of your toddler should do the same thing, so your child doesn't get mixed messages. Create a plan ahead of time and write it down so Dad, Grandma, the folks at day care, and others all know what to do—and what not to do.

- **A time-out.** I know it sounds like I'm contradicting myself, but there's a point where persistence doesn't pay, and that point is when your toddler wants absolutely nothing to do with you or your silly potty training, even after days, weeks, or months of success. Sometimes you need a time-out from potty training because something rocked your toddler's world, such as a new baby, a move, divorce, a new day-care provider, or other life change. Or when, like me, you realize you started training before your toddler was truly ready. Whatever the reason, you might need to take a time-out for a while before you start up again later.

- **Patience.** Potty training can feel like a game of Chutes and Ladders. Just when you think you're nearing the end, you slide back down a few spaces. But setbacks are normal. Take my pee-on-a-plane incident, for example, which might be scarier than snakes on a plane. On a flight from Edmonton to Toronto one night, a father told me about how his son, who was sleeping on the seat between us, had been "completely potty trained" by age two. When the plane later sat on the tarmac during a lightning storm, I let the little boy sit on my lap and look out the window. Suddenly, I felt something warm and wet on my legs. So much for "completely." Luckily, I had packed fresh pants. Also, a sense of humor.

- **Sense of humor.** See above.

Will It Be a Dry Night?

DON'T EXPECT YOUR toddler to stay dry all night right away. It takes an average of eight months for a child to potty train fully, including nights. You can help matters by limiting the amount of fluids your toddler drinks before bedtime. (Yes, that means the bottle or sippy cup you secretly let him take to bed so he'll drift off without a fuss.) And make sure your toddler uses the potty before bedtime.

Okay, I admit it. . . .

"For me, [potty training] is the hardest part of parenting so far."

—*Alexis,*
Marysville, California

What if bedwetting becomes a habit, though? Experts say that some 15 percent of children still wet the bed after age three. More boys tend to wet the bed than girls, and it is hereditary, but it usually ends by puberty. Some kids simply sleep too soundly to notice, while others have accidents when they're under the weather. But if your toddler wets the bed, don't punish him. Just clean it up. If it happens often, consider putting him back into a training diaper at night, just in case.

Momma Said

WE ASKED: How long did it take to potty train your kids?

Several months: 43%
A week: 29%
Several weeks: 21%
A year or longer: 7%
One day: 0%
Several days: 0%

When Do I Call in Reinforcements?

IF YOU'VE GOT the pediatrician and your sister on speed dial, you probably know what to do. But if you're determined to figure out potty training all on your own because your mother managed to pull it off with six kids—on their first birthdays—even though they didn't have running water, and she didn't speak much English . . . and she tells you about it every time she sees your toddler in diapers, think again. It's okay to ask for help. Really. That's what chat rooms are for.

My neighbor's son had a toilet phobia that prompted him to hold in his poop for days until he was so constipated, he needed help. Somewhere along the way, probably at one of those loud, frightening public toilets that look like they could swallow an unsuspecting toddler, he got the idea that he was better off holding it in than sitting on the big, bad potty.

My neighbor called her pediatrician, who suggested suppositories and a clever mom-tested trick that ultimately worked. He told her to put her son on the potty in his training pants whenever he had to poop. After a few days, she secretly cut a hole in his training pants. When his poop hit the water, she told him, "See that? You're such a big boy, your poop is too strong for your Pull-Ups!" This brilliant idea worked, and he overcame his fear of the toilet.

If there's nothing left in your bag of tricks, call your pediatrician, your mom, or a friend who has potty trained a kid or two, or surf the Internet. There are loads of ideas (and commiseration) online. You never know which one will work for you.

Of course, if there's a physical problem, such as constipation or special needs, consult your child's pediatrician.

"My oldest refused to have a bowel movement on the potty. He would do it once or twice and then quit for days or weeks at a time. Finally, I gave him 'ownership' of his product, meaning that if he made it, he had to clean it up. One time, and he was completely trained."

It worked for me!

—*Kim, Slippery Rock, Pennsylvania*

WE ASKED: If you could outsource potty training your child, would you?

No: 53%
Yes: 47%

Gimme a break

Create a No-Poop Zone

When you're potty training, it can feel like your whole world is about pee and poop. Create your own No Poop Zone, a place where you can go and take a break from potty training while someone else monitors the Pull-Ups for a while. It can be a room in your house (with a door that locks), a hammock in the backyard, or the library, where you sit and read multisyllabic words all by yourself.

Just a Minute!

The Potty Training Blues

My toddler hides behind the couch

Whenever she's gotta pee.

I try to get her to go on the potty

But she pretends she can't see me.

I've got the potty training blues.

The wipes, the bribes, the stickers, the mess.

I gave up and put her in diapers, I confess.

I've got the potty training blues.

My toddler goes on the potty for my mother,

But won't go near the bathroom for me.

So I gave her an incentive—

A jumbo bag of M&M'S and a brand new Barbie.

I've got the potty training blues.

The wipes, the bribes, the stickers, the mess.

Sometimes I give her yet another Webkinz, I confess.

I've got the potty training blues.

My toddler's the only kid in diapers

At her karate class.

All the other moms like to remind me,

And it makes me feel like an. . . .

I've got the potty training blues.

The wipes, the bribes, the stickers, the mess.

Sometimes I lie about our potty success.
I've got the potty training blues.
The wipes, the bribes, the stickers, the mess.
You can get her to go? Wow, I'm impressed.
I've got the potty training blues.
Oh yeah.

Chapter Five

Your New Gated Community:
Keeping Your Toddler Safe in and Outside the Home

 WE ASKED: What's the hardest part about having a toddler?

"EEK! The abundance of energy and that they are into what seems like *everything*!"

—Jennifer, Fayetteville, Arkansas

It is all our fault. While my sister-in-law was in the bathroom, the rest of the family encouraged my then sixteen-month-old nephew to run through the kitchen to the family room and then to the dining room and back through the kitchen in one big, increasingly fast circle through my mother-in-law's house. My internal Mommy Monitor was sounding: "Warning! Accident ahead!" But I figured that the other grown-ups had it covered, so I said nothing. Sure enough, he wiped out in the dining room, clocking his head, creating a walnut-size purple and red bump on his forehead.

While he cried hysterically in his grandmother's arms, my sister-in-law returned from the bathroom. "You?" she said to me. "I didn't think you'd let something like this happen." She was right. I should have heeded my Mommy Monitor and stopped the whirling dervish before he dove headfirst into the doorjamb. So what can you do to protect your toddler—and your stuff—even when everyone else doesn't? Here we'll take a look at toddler-proofing beyond the safety gates and toilet latches. It's the real-world way to make sure your house and your toddler are safe.

Lock Up the Stuff— There's a Toddler in the House

WHEN HER KIDS were little, one of my neighbors had a room full of nothing but toys—no tables to knock over, no chairs to climb, no window treatments to pull down onto the dog, who was just trying to get a little nap in the sun—just toys, and lots of them. I'm sure that when she set up her wedding registry, she never pictured having an entire room done in Early Playskool, but she did, and it worked for her and her toddlers. It was a safe place for the kids to play, and a room where Mom could finally, blessedly, let down her guard just a bit, never once wondering, *Was that crash the fireplace pokers or my laptop?*

But you don't have to dedicate a room to toddlerhood to make your house and the stuff in it safe from grubby little hands. Here's how.

Baby-Proofing Is Not Enough Anymore

IT WAS KIND of cute how your hubby went through the house sticking plug covers into outlets and putting a lock on the cabinet under the kitchen sink when your baby wasn't even old enough to roll over, wasn't it? But now that your toddler is mobile and messy, you need to take a second look at what you thought was "child-proofing." Go through your home room by room—and don't skip the rooms set off by safety gates, because you never know when your toddler will figure out how to climb them or open them. Think like a toddler looking for trouble, and you'll be able to toddler-proof your house pretty well.

Also, keep your purse out of reach. Toddlers love to play in Mom's purse, but it can contain many hazards, such as coins, makeup, and prescription medications. Besides, think about where the bottom of your purse has been. It's probably carrying more germs than the ball pit at your local play center.

Okay, I admit it. . . .

"I wanted to break a lease after moving into a rental house that I hadn't seen. The landlord had assured me the house was child-proofed, but it was not. The house was virtually impossible to block entry into the kitchen and whatnot, and my son climbs over gates. He told me to take a parenting class."

—*Angela, Clearwater, Florida*

Ten Ways to Toddler-Proof Your House Right Now

1. **Look at what's hanging.** If there's a string hanging down—like the cord to your blinds or the switch for a lamp, your toddler may well yank it. Roll up cords out of your toddler's reach to avoid strangulation.

2. **Block the stairs.** Don't just close the door leading to the basement stairs. Make sure your toddler can't open it by locking the doorknob, installing a bolt that's out of his reach, or placing a plastic cover over the doorknob. Beware of the latter, because I've heard of some clever toddlers figuring out how to bypass them.

3. **Use safety gates.** If your stairs don't have doors, install gates at the top and/or bottom. Even if your toddler can get over them, they'll slow her down.

4. **Cover your outlets.** We even covered plugs in the vacation house we rented. You never know when a toddler will

> ## Okay, I admit it. . . .
>
> "I think I should go on the record and say that in my experience with four kids that they are generally suicidal for the first few years of life, and it becomes our responsibility to keep them from killing themselves. I say 'suicidal,' because let's face it: toddlers are always trying to kill themselves by choking on things they put in their mouths, hitting their heads, falling down, running out in front of cars, messing with pets, testing Mom's patience, you name it!"
>
> — *Colleen, Tucson, Arizona*

sneak under a table and start sticking various objects in the outlets while you wonder where he went.

5. **Duct tape the remote.** In fact, tape up anything within reach that has an easy-to-open battery latch. Don't assume that everyone in your family will always remember to put the remote out of reach. Double-A and triple-A batteries are oh-so-slender, fitting up toddler noses and—especially scary—down their throats.

6. **Pad the table corners.** Take it from someone who got four-teen stitches next to her eye thanks to a sharp coffee table corner: protect your toddler by padding your furniture. (If only you could protect your furniture by padding your toddler.)

7. **Move your pet's food and litter box out of reach.** According to your toddler, kibble fits nicely up the nose or in the ears, and the water bowl is a great place for all sorts of things, including your BlackBerry. Move them before he finds that out.

8. **Sweat the small stuff.** If it's smaller than his elbow, put it out of reach. This includes (but is not limited to): coins, erasers, staples, screws, nails (and anything that's stored in small plastic bins at Home Depot), rubber bands, keys, packing peanuts, real peanuts and other edible choking hazards, marbles, buttons, and any other small items you've stuffed into the junk drawer.

9. **Secure the big wobbly things.** Imagine which appliances or furniture would tip over on a rocky boat, and you've found some of the most dangerous items in your house. Latch bookshelves, lock up the oven door, and secure the TV. Don't put heavy items on top of furniture that your toddler can pull down on top of herself.

10. **Look up the plants.** Make sure none of the plants your toddler can reach are poisonous. You can easily find lists on the Internet, but some of the most popular outdoor plants that can cause problems are mums and hydrangea. Some popular indoor plants that can pose a danger include caladium, English ivy, and philodendron.

"The toddler stage definitely keeps you on your toes."

— *Mary, Chicago, Illinois*

It worked for me!

"We turned the formal dining room into a playroom by putting large baby gates on both doorways. The kids could play in a contained, safe environment, and I could (in theory) go to the bathroom in peace."

—*Chrissy, Dillsburg, Pennsylvania*

Prevent Poisoning

YOU MAY THINK you've locked up every potential poison in the house, but think again. One of my neighbors had to call Poison Control when her toddler ate some of the baby's diaper rash ointment, which, of course, wasn't secured behind safety latches. It was on the diaper changing table, where we've all kept diaper rash ointment.

Have you ever lost a pill under the heater? I'll bet tiny toddler fingers could retrieve it. Have you ever rushed off to help a kid while you're in the middle of cleaning? Did you take the toilet cleaner with you? Probably not. Do you know what's in every corner of your garage? Your toddler will find out for you.

I don't mean to scare you, but it's probably a good idea to keep the phone number for Poison Control by each telephone. Program it into your cell, too. The American Association of Poison Control Centers will direct your call to your local center automatically when you call (800) 222-1222. Here's what you'll need to tell them:

• How much your toddler weighs.

• Any medical conditions he or she has.

• What medications he or she takes.

• A description of what your toddler swallowed. If it's from a bottle, read them the ingredients. If it's a plant, be prepared to describe it.

Chuck the Ipecac

The American Academy of Pediatrics now recommends that parents throw out their syrup of ipecac, once recommended as a home treatment for poisoning by inducing vomiting. A study published in a medical journal showed that ipecac didn't reduce the need for children to visit the ER, nor did it improve their outcomes. Also, some poisons do more harm when vomited. Leave it to the medical professionals to figure out the best way to get it out of your toddler.

Poisons Here, There, and Everywhere

Not everything that's poisonous has a skull and crossbones printed on its label. You may have poisons you're not even aware of. Other items aren't necessarily poisonous but can cause problems if ingested by a toddler. Here's a list of things you need to lock up right now.

In the kitchen, laundry area, or linen closet:

- Furniture polish
- Bleach
- Lye
- Bug killers
- Boric acid
- Disinfectants
- Detergents
- Spray starches

- Rug cleaners
- Floor cleaners
- Oven cleaners

In the bath:

- Toxic essential oils, such as camphor, wintergreen oil, and sassafras
- Bleach
- Prescription and over-the-counter medications
- Iron tablets
- Rubbing alcohol
- Nail polish remover
- Shaving cream
- Certain soaps
- Makeup
- Toilet bowl cleaners

In the garage:

- Gasoline
- Kerosene
- Antifreeze
- Paint and paint thinners
- Turpentine
- Weed killers

Safety Devices or Marketing Gimmicks?

HERE'S A RECIPE for safety item purchasing blunders: A cranky, hungry, pregnant woman with a shopping cart in the safety section at Babies "R" Us. That's how come I ended up with two toilet latches that my toddlers quickly unlatched permanently and a corner table bumper that doesn't fit on oval coffee tables. But other safety gadgets have turned out to be very useful deterrents for toddler trouble. What should you buy?

Maybe you have one of those kids who stays right where you put her. My cousin had a toddler like this. She sat a lot, so I gave her a SIT 'N SPIN for Christmas. *If she's gonna sit, she oughta spin,* I thought, as I chased my boys through the store. But for the rest of us, there's more work involved. And you're better off overgadgeting the house than finding out the hard way that your toddler likes to open the scissors drawer.

Five Must-Have Safety Gadgets

1. **Safety gates.** Even if your toddler figures out how to get over them like a suspect on *Cops*, it'll slow her down so you can grab her before she gets to the other side. Average price: $12 to $40.

2. **Antiscald device.** Considering my older son climbed into the sink and turned the water on, this one's a must. It regulates water temperature on your faucets to help prevent scalding. Average price: $5 to $30.

3. **Door stops, doorknob covers, and door locks.** These will help keep your kids inside or out of rooms where they don't belong. Door stops help keep your toddler's fingers from getting pinched. Average price: $1 to $5 each. Put them in high traffic areas and in your toddler's room.

4. **Smoke and carbon monoxide detectors.** Some states have regulations that specify where such detectors must be placed, so check them out. Carbon monoxide detectors are recommended for houses with gas or oil heat or attached garages.

5. **Safety latches and locks.** While the toilet latches turned out to be a bust for us, the drawer latches and cabinet locks were very helpful in our house.

"While 'yes' is wonderful, it's still okay and important to say 'no.'"

—*Emmie, Utica, New York*

It worked for me!

WE ASKED: What do you wish someone had told you about parenting toddlers before you had them?

"You think you know, but you have no idea. Get ready for the toughest job you'll ever have."

—*Lisa, Somerset, New Jersey*

Welcome to Hazard Minefield:
Watch Your Step—And Your Toddler

On Christmas, I was my sister-in-law's secret informant.

"Lit candle in the bathroom," I whispered.

She disappeared, and when I later walked past my in-laws' powder room, I noticed that the candle had been blown out.

"Grapes on the coffee table," I advised.

Suddenly, the grape bowl was relocated to the dining room table.

"Red wine, three o'clock," I said, but my husband grabbed the wine glass before our nephew could knock it over onto the white couch, or worse, stick his tongue in it.

When you're the mother of a toddler, it's like being in the Secret Service: your job is to notice and remove hazards that few others seem to recognize. And you're on duty 24/7. Here are some tips on how to sweep someone else's house for potential safety hazards before your toddler finds them for you.

Scan the hors d'oeuvres. If you don't have a toddler in your house anymore, you might forget that a plate full of nuts, grapes, shrimp, chips, and so on pose a potential choking hazard for a toddler while Mommy turns her head for just a second to say, "I'll just have water, please."

Don't lurch for the dish, screaming, "She's gonna choke!" as though you've just spotted an explosive device in the living room. Your host or hostess might get offended, and with good reason. Instead, say, "I'm going to save your floor, couch, and sanity by putting this out of my toddler's reach." Then you can all chuckle while you surreptitiously scan the room for more hazards, like the cords hanging from the blinds, for example.

Check the doors. My in-laws have a door at the top of the stairs to the basement that we've all monitored over the years. Admittedly, it was easier to keep it shut when we just had two toddlers and a baby to watch over. But now that they're older, my boys sometimes forget to shut the door when they rush downstairs to play on the oh-so-cool swing my father-in-law installed in the basement. And my nephew just loves to follow the big kids—right to the edge of those perilous stairs.

Stake out all the doors leading to possible dangers and close them. The doors might not stay closed, especially at a large gathering where ("Sorry, Sis. I didn't see him get by me") booze is being served and/or older children are running free. In that case, it's best to make a mental note of the most dangerous doors and learn to move quickly when your toddler heads in their direction.

Hide the breakables. Is there a vase sitting on top of a stereo speaker? You could spend the entire party monitoring the vase, or you could move the darn thing, just in case. There's nothing wrong with toddler-proofing your hostess's fine breakables while protecting your toddler from potential harm. Chances are, she didn't even think of its hazardous, perilous positioning on top of the speaker until your toddler started hammering at it with her shoe.

Put out fires. Though my kids managed not to set themselves ablaze with the three beautiful candles in an empty room at my brother's family gathering, they did get the hot wax all over his brand-new hardwood floors. I felt like saying, "I'll just have the migraine medicine and a nap, please."

Candles are festive and pretty and all that stuff, but they are purveyors of *fire*. And fire is not a friend to your toddler, even if it's in a cutesy Hallmark votive designed to look like Rudolph's nose all lit up. What toddler wouldn't want to touch that or any other glowing object?

The elder generation might insist that they were able to light candles and leave them out when you were a child, blah, blah, blah. But the older generation let us sit at the edge of the road while we ate Pop Rocks and inhaled fumes from leaded gas. Don't defer to them on this one. Just blow out the candles and blame it on the wind.

Don't get liquored up. If there's ever been anyone who could use a drink, it's someone who has chased after a toddler who bolted—once again—past a long line of people at the bank for the basket of lollipops. But don't drink—not in someone else's house. Downing (or even, sipping) a glass of wine or two while you're on duty, combined with sleep deprivation, fatigue, and a secret desire to run away to Key West until the kids are old enough for kindergarten, is like drugging the watch dog outside FBI headquarters. It only takes a second for your toddler to figure which door leads to the great outdoors.

"For things like scaling furniture, I remove them from what they are doing. If I can, I find a suitable alternative for them to climb on, like pillows on the floor."

—*Julie, West Chester, Pennsylvania*

WE ASKED: What do you wish someone had told you about parenting toddlers?

"I wish I had known how much patience and stamina I was going to need."

—*Lisa, Blue Bell, Pennsylvania*

Weather Warnings

JUST WHEN YOU thought you had your toddler all figured out, the season changes, and you've got a whole new set of safety hazards to monitor or eliminate altogether. What can you expect when leaf piles near the road and baseboard heaters on high in the house are replaced by trippy sandals and water, water everywhere as the hazard du jour or vice versa?

Spring and Summertime Stakes

In our lake community, we know all too well how fast a kid can disappear near water. Luckily, we've found our missing children on land, chasing a butterfly, rushing to the playground, or sitting not five feet away, playing quietly while we coax our hearts out of our throats.

But drowning is one of the leading causes of death for young children. The Centers for Disease Control reports that most young children who drowned in pools were:

- Last seen inside the home
- Missing less than five minutes
- Cared for by one or both parents at the time

Here are some tips for reducing the chance for accidental drowning:

- **Swimming pools.** If you own a pool, enclose it with a fence that's at least four feet high with a self-latching gate and install pool alarms. Empty and turn upside-down kiddie pools when they're not in use. Monitor your kids like a momma hawk.

- **Other water hazards.** Even if you don't own a pool, consider potential water hazards in your area, including a neighbor's pool; ponds, streams, or other small bodies of water; a hot tub in your yard or in someone else's; an area that floods easily after storms; a bucket left outside in the rain, and so on. Inside the house, drain your bathtub as soon as you're done with it, and never leave your toddler unattended in the tub.

• **Lakes, rivers, oceans.** Don't rely on lifeguards to monitor your toddler for you. They have to watch dozens of people at once, while you just have your toddler and your other kids. It's especially hard to see people underwater in anything but a chlorinated pool or hot tub, so stay very close to your toddler on beach outings.

Remember, it only takes an inch-and-a-half of water to drown a child.

Fun in the Sun?

The good news is that once your child is six months old, you can start using sunscreen. The bad news is that once your child can walk, it gets increasingly more difficult to make your toddler stand still for the pre-sun slathering.

I only had to chase my toddlers around the beach with a glob of sunscreen on my hand once before I learned a valuable lesson: apply sunscreen at home. Even now that they're big boys, we slather up at home, so I don't have to compete with their friends, the water, or anything else that makes it difficult to get them to stay in one place very long. It's the only chance I can get my own skin completely covered as well.

Experts will tell you to make sure your toddler wears a hat in the sun. Ha ha ha ha ha! It's near impossible to keep a hat on a toddler, especially when it appears to hinder her ability to chase the seagulls off the sand. Try and try and try to get a hat on your toddler as many times as you can before you make her irate and cranky.

Otherwise, stay off the beach when the sun's rays are at their strongest, between 10:00 AM and 2:00 PM. That's usually nap time and lunchtime, anyhow. Also, reapply the sunscreen often and stay in the shade whenever you can.

Playground Predicaments

It's amazing any of us made it to adulthood in one piece. On my school's playground, there was a set of metal monkey bars that—amazingly—didn't burn anyone's fingers, knock out any teeth, break any ribs, or bonk us unconscious. I have no idea how we survived that accident trap, but I noticed it's since been replaced by much safer equipment.

Still, not all playgrounds are completely safe for your toddler. In fact, many playgrounds are designed for older kids, so you need to be extra careful when you bring your toddler along. Here are some hazards to look for on the playground:

- Bigger kids who can trample or knock over your toddler as they race through like a herd of buffalo
- Hardware that sticks out and can clip your toddler
- Tripping hazards, like concrete footings or other kids' toys
- Splinters on wood playground sets
- Guardrails designed for taller kids (your toddler could slip through)
- Hot metal or even plastic on a hot, sunny day
- Puddles, broken glass, animal poop
- Half-bucket seats on swings, because your toddler can fall out of them

- Drawstrings or hoods on your toddler's clothes that can get caught on slides

WE ASKED: What do you wish someone had told you about parenting toddlers?

"That gray hairs would pop out of my head like wildfire!"

—*Danelle, Middleburg Heights, Ohio*

Winter Worries

If you live in a cold climate, you've got some extra safety concerns come winter. Even though your toddler probably isn't snowboarding his way down the hill in your backyard (yet), you still need to consider certain winter safety issues:

- **Prevent frostbite.** Maybe you were lucky enough to find matching mittens this morning, but you need to make sure that they (a) stay on your toddler's hands, and (b) stay dry. If you're out in the cold for any extended period of time, check your toddler's hands for those mittens. I kept extra pairs in my car and diaper bag, just in case. You can find cheap mittens at most stores like Wal-Mart.

- **Dress your toddler warmly.** My best friend received eight snowsuits for her infant as baby shower gifts. But when her daughter was a toddler, she was on her own to make sure she had one. When my son was potty training in December, though, I skipped the one-piece snowsuit and got him a separate coat and snow pants. For most trips in the car, however, he didn't need the pants unless we were headed snow-tubing or sledding. On very cold days, your best bet is to dress your toddler in layers and make sure he doesn't ditch his hat when you're not looking.

• **Use protective gear for outdoor activities.** I've always made my kids wear their ski or bike helmets when they go sledding. Think about it: you're sending (or riding with) your toddler down a hill at speeds faster than she can run. If she comes in contact with something (a tree, a fence, her brother), wouldn't you want her head to be protected?

• **Beware of icy walkways.** It's hard enough to walk on ice when you're an expert walker. But imagine how hard it is when you've just learned how to put one foot in front of the other. Make sure the walkways outside your home are ice-free before you let your toddler walk on them. And don't think you can carry your toddler and walk on ice without potentially landing on your arm, your butt, or your kid. One solution for when you're faced with an icy walk is to put down two towels or two large pieces of cardboard. Walk on one and then put down the other. Repeat. Your toddler will think it's a game—to you, a long and tedious game, but at least it's a safe one.

Holiday Hazards

Ho, Ho, Ho . . . no! While the holidays can bring in cheer and fun, they're also more work for you. Here are some holiday hazards to consider when you're entertaining at home or out and about:

- Holly and mistletoe are poisonous plants, so keep them out of reach. Contrary to popular belief, poinsettias pose a danger only if your toddler eats hundreds of their leaves.

- Breakable ornaments are enticing and dangerous.

- Oh, how I hated candles when my kids were toddlers. If you light them, keep a very close eye on them, especially on your menorah. Never leave it lit and unattended with a toddler in the house. If you have to, use the lightbulb version.

- If you host a party, keep the alcoholic drinks and cigarette butts out of your toddler's hands by regularly clearing out leftover glasses and ashtrays (I recommend not smoking near children at all; as far as I'm concerned, when you smoke, your kids smoke, too).

Year-Round Hazards

Finally, keep in mind these hazards that you might not have thought about:

- **Balloons.** They are a choking hazard for kids under three. Don't let your toddler attempt to blow one up, and keep an eye out for broken balloons at parties. Throw them out immediately. I've walked around parties, stuffing popped balloons in my pockets. It looks strange, but the other parents appreciate my janitorial services.

• **Shopping carts.** Your toddlers can climb out of the cart when you've turned to check the price on a gallon of milk. Use the cart's safety belt, and never leave your toddler unattended in a shopping cart. If he's too fidgety to sit still, don't put him in the cart at all, but be prepared to put things back on low shelves and to apologize to other shoppers a lot.

• **Bunk beds.** They're just too high for such little kids. Even if your toddler's bed is on the bottom, she might try to climb up to the top just like her big sister. Skip the bunk beds until she's old enough to safely get in and out of them without your supervision.

> **It worked for me!**
>
> "I have found that it is much more productive to redirect my son when he does something he shouldn't."
>
> —Gretchen, Winder, Georgia

Gimme a break

Take a Real Coffee Break

If you find yourself filling any spare moment with chores, you're never going to get a real break. Spend nap time watching your favorite TV show, reading a magazine, talking to a friend on the phone, sleeping, or whatever recharges you. The dishes in the sink can wait. Really.

Just a minute!

See the Amazing Escaping Toddler!

. . . *who can* hurdle a safety gate with more air than
Marion Jones at the Olympics!

. . . *who can* escape a playpen faster than a husband in
the bra department at JC Penney's!

. . . *who can* unlatch a toilet lock as effortlessly as a
die-hard Red Sox fan flips open a beer on game day!

. . . *who can* slither out of a high chair—
safety strap and all—more hastily
than a mud slide moves a mansion in Malibu!

. . . *who can* pull the plug on the baby monitor
faster than Simon Cowell
can shut down a singer's career!

Seeing is believing.

Come see for yourself the Amazing Escaping Toddler!

Chapter Six

Beyond Mac 'n' Cheese:
Feeding Your Toddler

"Don't compromise. If they don't eat it, they'll be really hungry at the next meal."

—*Sara, Layton, Utah*

It worked for me!

Two Different Toddlers,
Two Different Palates

My toddler was looking at us as though we'd all lost our minds. My family was eating lobsters on the patio behind my parents' house while Nicholas, who'd just turned two, furrowed his brow. He pointed at the odd creatures on our plates, tilted his head, and said, "Orange bugs?" He has never eaten a lobster—or much of anything else. Now a tween, he's still a picky eater, even if the food doesn't look like big insects.

My younger son, on the other hand, has a more mature—and expensive—palate. As a toddler, when Chris discovered his family eating lobsters on the deck during a summer vacation, he sidled up to me to ask for a bite. Soon, he asked for another and another. "More monster. More monster," he demanded. Nowadays, he gets a lobster every birthday and a few times in between. While his brother still turns up his nose at most foods, Chris eats just about anything I serve him. If only I could bottle his enthusiasm for food that's good for you, then I'd be a billionaire.

Whether you have a picky eater or a lobster lover, you're no doubt concerned with what to feed your toddler now that he's outgrown the oh-so-easy baby food. Here's what you should consider when it comes to your toddler and food.

Bye-Bye Baby Food: Introducing the Good Stuff

I COULDN'T WAIT for my sons to start eating grown-up food, so I could ditch the baby food jars and just make one meal for all of us. I assumed that my older son, who had chowed his way through his first year and looked like he was destined to play linebacker for Nebraska, would take to our food just like he had adored his strained peas. But when he turned one, he promptly lost interest in food. All I could get into him without a fuss were Cheerios, cookies, and juice. He pretty much ate like he had just given blood.

If your toddler suddenly becomes a picky eater, don't worry. He's not growing as fast as he did during his first year, so he doesn't need as many calories. As long as he's active and growing, he'll be okay. But that doesn't mean you should feed him a steady diet of Mint Milanos and Mott's, either.

Experts say that toddlers need about 1,300 calories a day. It doesn't sound like a lot, especially considering your toddler is probably running around much of the day, burning up calories as he races through your pachysandra. But he's little, and his food servings should be much smaller than yours, about one-quarter to one-half of what's on your plate, or roughly an ounce or so.

What Should Go on Your Toddler's Plate?

IF YOU HAD asked my older son what a toddler should eat, the answer would have been one chicken nugget and seventeen animal crackers. My younger son would have preferred the lobster bisque and half the rolls in the basket. But it wasn't up to my toddlers what to eat. I had to come up with something that satisfied both of their eating habits as well as my nutritional concerns for them.

You could end up obsessing over every calorie that does (or doesn't) go into your toddler's tummy, but that serves no one any good. In fact, experts say that toddlers' appetites are notoriously fickle. One meal they eat like a rugby player during playoffs, and the next, they nibble on a grilled cheese sandwich and call it a day. The good news is that this is normal.

The experts' guidelines on what to feed your toddler are, in my opinion, a bit unrealistic. The recommended six servings of grains translates into six halves of bread for a one-year-old or three cups of pasta for a two-year-old. Unless they're training for an Iron Man competition or something, I don't know any toddlers who can eat all that plus the recommended five to ten servings of vegetables and fruit, three servings of milk, and two to three servings of protein (meat, eggs, peanut butter) in one day.

But what your toddler eats in one day is less important than what he or she eats over a period of days or weeks. If you get half an egg, some whole grain bread, and a handful of strawberries into your toddler at breakfast, congratulations! But don't expect lunch and dinner to necessarily be as much a success. Instead, look at what your toddler eats in a few days or weeks and adjust meals according to his nutritional intake over time, rather than just in a day's worth of meals.

Also, keep trying to give your toddler new foods, even if he shunned peas yesterday and the day before and Saturday, too. It takes an average of ten introductions for a kid to take to a new food. Still, some kids simply never like certain foods.

I've always made sure that my picky eater gets protein and a veggie or a fruit that he picks out at each meal. He's always taken a multivitamin (conveniently disguised as gummy bears) each day, and he never gets any dessert until he eats the good stuff first. Though he's built more like a swimmer than a football player now, he still does love his desserts. The orange bugs? Not at all.

"Cover it with either ketchup or cheese. Works every time."

—*Whitney, Bridgewater, Virginia*

It worked for me!

"Only give them one bite of the 'yucky' stuff, and once it's tried and swallowed, then they may have the rest of their plate filled."

—*Angie, Indianapolis, Indiana*

It worked for me!

Don't Get Juiced

DON'T LET YOUR toddler's sippy cup fill him up. He needs only about 300–400 calories of cow's or breast milk a day and—brace yourself—less than 100 calories of juice per day. That's about one sippy cup full of what was my son's favorite elixir for years until he quit cold turkey in fourth grade. Don't fool yourself into thinking that if you give your toddler the 100 percent juice, it's okay to let him suck down a few dozen ounces of it a day, either. Juice is sugar, and lots of sugar isn't good for anyone.

Food Allergies

ABOUT 2 TO 6 percent of children have food allergies, some of them severe. Half of toddlers who develop food allergies outgrow them by their seventh birthdays. As your toddler is exposed to more new foods, you might be concerned that she might join the seemingly growing ranks of kids who can't eat certain foods.

When my neighbor's son comes over, I'm especially careful to wipe down the table and counters if I've eaten something that could trigger his nut allergies. But how do you know if your toddler—or your neighbor's toddler—is allergic to certain foods? Trial and error. Here's how to spot a food allergy.

Signs and Symptoms of Food Allergies

- Watery eyes

- Hives

- Runny nose

- Trouble breathing

- Chronic eczema

- Bloody diarrhea

- Swelling of the head and/or neck

Symptoms can appear minutes or hours after ingestion. Obviously, if your toddler is in distress, call 911. But for mild symptoms, report the incident to your pediatrician, who will probably advise you to remove the potential allergen from your toddler's diet for two weeks and then reintroduce it to see if it produces the same effect. If, like my neighbor's son, your toddler has reactions to several foods, or if you're having a hard time identifying the culprit, your pediatrician may refer you to a specialist who can run tests to help identify which foods your toddler is allergic to.

Should You Go Organic?

ORGANIC FOODS ARE grown without pesticides, hormones, and antibiotics. It's certainly easier, not to mention cheaper, to buy nonorganic foods, but consider this: children are more likely to absorb the harmful effects of pesticides, which may cause all sorts of serious illnesses, including immune disorders, reproductive problems, and cancer. Plus, pesticides can block the good effects of foods, keeping your toddler's body from absorbing certain vitamins and nutrients.

But before you run around the kitchen, feverishly throwing out all of your food, think about which foods your toddler eats the most of and the most often, and consider going organic there first. If buying organic proves too costly, you might want to grow your own fruits and vegetables at home or join an organic co-op or buying club, where you use the power of bulk buying to drive prices down.

Here's a list of the foods found to have the most pesticides, the so-called "Dirty Dozen":

1. Strawberries

2. Bell peppers

3. Spinach

4. Cherries

5. Peaches

6. Cantaloupe

7. Celery

8. Apples

9. Apricots

10. Green beans

11. Grapes

12. Cucumbers

The least contaminated produce includes eggplant, broccoli, sweet peas, cabbage, avocados, pineapples, mangoes, kiwi, and bananas.

The Environmental Protection Agency sets limits on the amount of pesticide residue permitted on local and imported food. They warn parents that children tend to consume larger quantities of milk, applesauce, and orange juice per pound of body weight than do adults. As a result, any pesticide-treated food that your child eats large quantities of has a greater potential for harm.

What About Peanut Butter?

The United States Department of Agriculture's annual food testing has found that 30 percent of peanut butters tested showed "detectable residues" of pesticides. But if your toddler is a Skippy or Jif lover, you may have a hard time selling him on the organic stuff, which tends to be less smooth and not as sweet. If you shop around, though, you can find a decent organic peanut butter. I have discovered that the organic peanut butter that doesn't have a layer of oil at the top of the jar is a good substitute. Just cut its thickness with extra jelly until your toddler gets used to the organic peanut butter's taste and consistency.

And Cow's Milk?

Most of the European Union, Canada, and Japan are among the countries that have banned the use of rBST, a synthetic bovine growth hormone dairy farmers inject in cows to increase milk production. Some critics say rBST increases the risk of cancer among consumers, but those claims have not been proven. The U.S. Food and Drug Administration says that milk treated with rBST is safe for consumers.

But some studies have shown rBST increases another cow hormone, IGF-1, which has been linked with increases in various types of cancer in humans. Plus, rBST can increase the chances for udder infections in cows, prompting the need for antibiotics, which ultimately end up in the milk you drink.

Frankly, the whole thing gives me a headache. Though organic milk is indeed pricey, I have made the switch for my family. Luckily, my supermarket's automatic coupon machine frequently gives me $1 coupons at checkout for either of the two types of organic milk it sells. Plus, the dairy farms offer free printable coupons online.

How Much Milk Is Too Much?

Cow's milk is a good source of calcium and vitamin D, and, when used correctly, can "do a body good," as the commercial used to say. But your toddler can drink too much milk. If she's drinking upward of forty-eight ounces of whole milk a day, she's ingesting about 900 calories *just from milk*—and she likely consumes only about 1,300 calories total each day. Some kids who fill up on milk often eat less food, thereby missing out on nutrients that aren't in milk, especially iron, and that can lead to anemia.

Your one- to two-year-old should drink about sixteen to twenty-four ounces of milk a day. And that's whole milk, because your toddler needs the fat for growth and development. (Don't you wish we moms needed more fat, too?)

If your toddler is allergic to cow's milk, or just plain doesn't like it, soy milk is a good alternative. Make sure it's whole soy milk, not fat-reduced or fat-free, and that it's fortified with vitamin A, vitamin D, and calcium. Soy milk is plant-based, so it doesn't have vitamin B_{12} in it, but you can make sure your toddler gets enough B_{12} in her breakfast cereal.

I have found some soy milk tastes pretty bad, so you'll need to taste test a few of them before you find one your family will drink. My kids and I like the vanilla-flavored kind the best.

If you're transitioning from formula to milk, take it one bottle at a time. I mixed the formula with increasing amounts of milk for a few days until, eventually, my toddlers had all milk in their bottles. Other moms make the switch cold turkey and never go back. You might want to switch to milk before you wean your toddler off the bottle and onto the sippy cup or, for the daring few, regular cups. That way, you won't inflict two major changes on your toddler at the same time. You know your toddler best, so decide what works for you.

Still Breast-Feeding?

IF YOU'RE STILL breast-feeding your toddler, note that his sessions might get shorter as he gets older. He's still getting nutrients from your breast milk, but "grown-up" food is supplying more of his vitamins now.

Many moms keep nursing toddlers for the emotional benefits and the convenience, though some have faced a stigma in our society—you know, those amazed stares and the "You're still breast-feeding?" comments. Some moms fight peer pressure to quit and keep on nursing at least once or twice a day well into toddlerhood. But some find it harder to wean a toddler. The bottom line is that you need to do what's best for you and your toddler, no matter what the other mommies say or how they look at you on the playground.

It worked for me!

"Lately, I say that the Broccoli Fairy (or, Whatever Food I Want Them to Eat Fairy) is coming. Then I cover my eyes and sing, 'Twinkle twinkle little star, how I wonder what you are.' When I uncover my eyes, the fairy has come and eaten that particular food. Of course, I am peeking to make sure they take a bite of the food. Then I make a big deal that the fairy came and took a bite of the food. I have no clue why this works, but it does!"

—*Danelle, Middleburg Heights, Ohio*

WE ASKED: Any tips for getting toddlers to eat what you put in front of them?

"Don't make a big deal out of it."

—*Bobbie, Saddle River, New Jersey*

Picky Eaters, Sneaky Snackers, and Other Toddler Eating Issues

As I MENTIONED, my older son is still a picky eater. I'm waiting for puberty to hit, because, certainly, no teenage boy would prefer to eat just a handful of cheese and a pickle for dinner, right? But I've learned a thing or two about feeding picky eaters along the way. Here are some things that have worked for me and may help you get the right foods into your toddler:

- **Give her a choice.** I've long offered a variety of foods to see what my son will eat. I don't mean that you should become a short-order cook. Rather, have your toddler choose between, say, lettuce and peas or apple sauce and canned pears before you make dinner. Sometimes, picky eaters are picky because they want control. If you give them a choice, however small, they'll feel in control.

- **Hold a taste test.** I've lined up a small sample of a variety of foods and asked my son to try a little of each one. If your toddler refuses, offer a small treat between each taste, such as a Skittle or Cheerios. Consider it "cleansing his palate" instead of the bribe that it is, and you'll likely take to it more easily. And so will he.

- **Never call it "yucky."** Even if you think broccoli is yucky, don't ever call it that. Instead, tell your toddler that nutritious foods are like gasoline for the car: she can't run without it.

- **Lock up the snacks.** If you let your toddler eat unlimited snacks or snack too close to meals, she'll likely eat less of the good stuff.

- **Withhold dessert.** Nobody gets the cookies, cake, or other treat for dessert until the nutritious foods go down.

- **Don't get into a battle of wills.** You can't force your toddler to eat, but you can control what's available to eat in your house. Don't make him sit at the table until he eats. You won't win that one. But do make sure there are a lot of good foods in your house and very few empty-calorie snacks so that when he does get hungry, the good stuff is there for him.

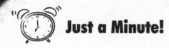 **Just a Minute!**

A Taste of Toddlerhood: Le Menu

HORS D'OEUVRES

Salad Frisée Aux "Dada"
A delightful mix of jumbled words,
in which only "Dada" can be heard clearly,
even though Mama is doing most of the work.

Petite Garçon Sur Countertop
In this surprising beginning to the meal,
our chef finds his way up where he doesn't belong—and the cat follows,
hoping something tasty will spill.

Dropsies en Croute
Le biter biscuit is on the high chair, and then on the floor,
and then on the high chair, and then on the floor, and then
on the high chair . . . Mon Dieu!

ENTRÉES
Shrieks Noisette
Like the Emergency Broadcasting Alarm, only louder and harder to turn off.

First Steps Confit
A wonderful main meal that goes well with
a side of relieved shoulders and free-at-last arms.

Chicken Nuggets Bordelaise
Because that's all you're going to be able to get into
her for the next eighteen months.

LES DESSERTS
Assortiment des Cusses
Enjoy our assortment of words you hope Grandma doesn't hear.

L'Aperitif
'Cause you're gonna need a drink.

Chapter Seven

You've Got a Friend:
Your Toddler's Playdates and Playgroups

WE ASKED: What's the best part about having a toddler?

"I got out of the house more and got involved with toddler things, like Kindermusic, playgroups, and things like that."

—*Angie, Hayden Lake, Idaho*

When our boys were toddlers, my neighbor Lynn and I had a saying: "It's not a playdate until someone's bleeding from the mouth." Maybe it was the vortex of energy from four toddlers that created hazards we simply couldn't see coming, but I swear that at every playdate our boys had, somebody wound up getting smacked in the mouth by accident. Once we had to get the ice pack out, we knew the playdate was officially over.

I'm not suggesting that your toddler's playdates will necessarily require visits to the ER or at least to the medicine cabinet. I'm just saying that playdates and playgroups can be full of surprises—some of them even good ones. Like when Lynn and I actually got to remain seated and finish complete sentences. What a day! We were giddy with excitement, like two people who had just discovered the swim-up bar at their Caribbean hotel.

One of the best parts about toddler playdates is that they give you a reason to leave home and, if you're lucky, talk to grown-ups. It's also a great way to teach your toddler socialization skills, such as "Share, share, that's fair" and "Don't hit Madison on the head with Elmo!" You almost never get to say things like that to adults. I mean, how many adults do you know named Madison?

Before you set out the Goldfish crackers and invite the neighbors over or sign up for Music Together class, you might want to consider a few things about your toddler's first friendships. I'll give you the inside scoop on toddlers' play—with or without the ice packs.

> **It worked for me!**
>
> "I would try to get out of the house and go to the park or an indoor play area. That way, I would usually end up having other moms to chat with, and my son could play nearby."
>
> —*Nicole, Woodlands, Texas*

Why Can't We Be Friends?

HAVE YOU EVER watched two fourteen-month-olds play together? They aren't actually playing *together* really. They often don't even talk to each other, but rather, to themselves, if they talk at all. In fact, they look like strangers at a salad bar. Meanwhile, you're wondering why you set up the playdate in the first place.

Younger toddlers are more likely to engage in what experts call "parallel play." In other words, they don't play *with* each other, just *next to* each other. Until they're about eighteen months old, chances are they'll hardly even acknowledge other children at a playdate, like curmudgeonly old men in their living rooms when it's time for *Jeopardy!* They want nothing to do with anyone else.

That's normal. Don't make suggestions on how to play. You don't have to sit the kids down in front of the Counting and Sorting Farm and say, "Hunter, show Austin where the cow goes." Hunter doesn't want to show Austin anything, and Austin doesn't care. And neither one of them wants to sit down, frankly, so go away, lady.

So what can you expect from your toddler's playdates?

Less than eighteen months old. The toddlers might get all excited to see each other and then promptly forget about each other to go play by themselves. You know, the sort of thing you see with the regulars at the slot machines in Vegas.

If the kids actually acknowledge that there's another toddler in the house, don't expect them to take turns, hold meaningful conversations, or listen to each other. They're just not ready for that sort of social interaction, no matter how much you try to facilitate it.

Please, put down the blocks and step away from the toddlers.

When your kids are less than eighteen months old, they just aren't ready for real play. Frankly, the playdate is for you. Sit down and enjoy the distraction for a while.

Eighteen months to three years old. Your toddler starts to understand that she's here to play with the other kids, and she may even want to. The kids start to interact with each other and even play with each other, sharing a toy, laughing, or chasing each other until someone trips and falls, and soon, everybody's crying—or not. You never know how it's going to go when toddlers play.

They may imitate each other's behavior, which is how my kids learned how to shoot hoops. Also, how to make fart noises with their mouths, thereby saving my brother the trouble.

They may even hug and kiss each other, so have the camera ready. What's a cute shot of two buddies embracing now is blackmail when they're in middle school.

Okay, I admit it. . . .

"Seventy percent of the time you are cleaning up after them."

—*Anne,*
West Milford, New Jersey

How to Host a Playdate/Playgroup Without Ticking Off Anyone

HERE'S THE DIRTY little secret about playdates: it's more about the mommies than anyone else. Unless you've got a sibling with a kid your toddler's age or a really, really good friend, chances are you're attending all of your toddler's playdates. Your role is part bodyguard, part roadie: you're there to protect your toddler from harm while providing her with whatever she needs to play.

But don't be fooled into thinking you can sink into a comfy chair with your coffee and dish dirt for an hour or two. Your parenting skills are on display and under scrutiny. If that doesn't concern you, go ahead and enjoy your bagel. But chances are, you want all the other mommies in your network to find out that you know what the hell you're doing. So be prepared to do a little refereeing and a little micromanaging at your toddler's playdates. Here's the job description of a playdate hostess:

- Provides healthful snacks, after checking for any nut or dairy allergies, aversions to anything nonorganic, and the attendance of vegans or vegetarians

- Disinfects (read: runs over with some wipes) toys prior to and after playdate

- Encourages sharing and fair play (that goes for the grown-ups, too)

- Fixes toys, video equipment, etc.

- Provides diaper changing area as needed; points out closest bathroom, which is clean and free of breakables, candles, and other toddler hazards, while providing adequate potty training supplies

- Has first-aid kit readily available, which includes, but is not limited to, boo-boo disinfectant, ice packs (unless you keep that in the freezer), and really cool Band-Aids featuring various popular cartoon characters

- Breaks up fights (again, for the grown-ups, too)

- Times the gathering around naps and school drop-offs and pick-ups for older siblings

The guests have their own responsibilities, such as:

- Bringing food, if asked

- Wrangling their own toddlers and helping to keep the peace among the kids—and the moms

- Helping to clean up the toys at the end of the playdate

- Properly discarding used diapers, tissues, and other waste generated by their toddlers or themselves

Keep the Peace

How do you make sure everyone is happy, safe, and busy in a room with small people who think the other small people might like to have their heads bounced with a mini basketball? Here are some tried-and-true playdate-hosting tips:

Don't bill it as the next big thing. If you blather on about how much fun the playdate/playgroup is going to be, your toddler will either get overly excited before it even begins or be terribly disappointed when his friend's mom calls to cancel due to sniffles and a cough that sounds like a Canada goose fighting over bread crusts. Don't tell her about the big event until no more than half an hour before it's scheduled to begin.

Avoid tug-of-wars. Don't set out your toddler's favorite brand-new toy and expect her to share it with her pal or pals. Hide it! Instead, put out toys with lots of parts, like blocks or jumbo Legos, or several of the same item, such as small trucks, dolls, or action figures.

Go big. It's easy to share something when it's big. Let the kids share space in a sandbox or take turns on a slide.

Don't rush in. If the kids start fighting over a toy, don't rush in to referee. Toddlers often have such short-term memories, they forget about the toy they just thought was the greatest thing since the Wiggles. If they start hitting or biting, though, call a foul on the play and swoop in to end the bad behavior. Don't expect your toddler to apologize to his friend and shake hands or hug after a tussle. If they fight, separate them and distract them with other toys, activities, or snacks. The older they get, the more effective a short time-out will work to teach them that fighting won't be tolerated.

Keep it short. Toddlers can stand to play with each other for an hour or two before they get cranky. And then the moms get cranky, too. Keep your playdates and playgroups brief.

Know when to fold. Sometimes, a playdate can go terribly awry, no matter how much you planned it out. The kids don't get along, somebody gets hurt, the other kid is terrified of your dog, or someone needs a nap. If you can't fix it with a snack, a change of scenery, or a short video, forget it. Even if your guest drove forty-five minutes to get to your house, politely suggest that you end the playdate and try again another time. Offer ideas where she can take her toddler on the way home, such as a playground or the local Starbucks. When everyone's crabby, there's no point in trying to force happiness into a miserable day.

Okay, I admit it. . . .

"A toddler-to-English dictionary would be nice."

—*Sara, Layton, Utah*

Playgroups are harder to break up, but when one mom calls it quits, the others often follow suit. Don't be afraid to leave your playgroup or to ask moms to wrap it up and go home.

Momma Said

WE ASKED: What's the best part about toddlers?

"They don't stay angry for long."

—*Julie, West Chester, Pennsylvania*

Meet on Neutral Ground

You've just met a nice mom at your toddler's Gymboree class. You want to invite her over for a playdate, but you're not sure your kids will get along, considering that your daughter is chatting up the teacher while her kid is clinging to Mommy's leg. You're not sure if her toddler is a wallflower or if she's just having a bad day. What can you do?

Invite her to meet you at a playground, Chuck E. Cheese, or a kid-friendly café. That way, if the kids don't get along, you can make an excuse to leave without shooing her out of your house.

Playgroups: That's a Whole Lotta Toddlers in One Place

WHETHER YOU HAVE a set weekly playgroup or a less-scheduled arrangement, a playgroup can be very important. Why? Because Mommy gets to talk to grown-ups. Oh, and it's helpful for your toddler to learn to socialize in a group, because eventually she'll go to school where she'll be expected to share toys and refrain from pushing Brianna in the face after she takes the last pink cupcake at the Valentine's party.

A playgroup can be the sanity saver you need on a long dreary day. Who doesn't need a change of scenery when you've been trapped inside with a toddler who's in the "Because why?" stage? And it's great for your toddler, too. She gets to play with new toys in fun locations with other like-minded folks who adore the Barney "Clean-Up" song as much as she does.

But how do you choose the right playgroup for you? Or do you start one yourself?

The Three Types of Playgroups

1. **Organized, paid groups.** More like classes than playgroups, these age-appropriate groups concentrate on one type of

activity, such as music, or a set of activities, as at Gymboree. A teacher leads the playgroup in songs, bubbles, and other engaging activities. Moms, dads, grandparents, and nannies participate in the activities by supervising their toddlers. In other words, you hold the parachute while singing, "The parachute goes up and down, up and down . . ." while you daydream about the Phish concerts you used to attend.

Pros: You don't have to plan or schedule anything, and you don't have to host a meeting. You just show up at a designated location every week. If your child misses a class, there are sometimes make-up classes to attend later. You can meet other moms with same-age kids and set up play-dates outside the group. It gets you out of the house, lets your toddler run off some energy, and, of course, you get to talk to adults.

Cons: Some classes can be costly—as much as a few hundred dollars for six to ten weeks of classes, especially if you're enrolling more than one child. As with any group setting, you can expose your toddler to all sorts of viruses and infections. And, if your toddler is having a rotten, no-good, miserable day, all the other mommies get to witness the meltdown.

2. **Organized, free groups.** These are less formal groups organized by a church, synagogue, mothers' group, or nonprofit organization. Some playgroups offer organized activities, crafts, and outings, such as to an amusement park or playground.

Pros: Groups are already organized, so you can simply sign up and show up. The cost is free, and, like paid playgroups, you have a reason to get out of the house. Groups are sometimes organized by similar interests, such as groups for working mothers, moms under thirty, religious affiliation, or parenting philosophies.

Cons: Sometimes, free playgroups fall victim to social politics. For example, one mom gets ticked off because another mom bad-mouthed breast-feeding, and suddenly a bunch of moms leave in a huff to start their own group. Meanwhile, your toddler is wondering what happened to his buddy Andrew who used to repeatedly open and close the door to the playhouse with him every Thursday morning.

3. **Mom-made, free groups.** More informal playgroups that often rotate meetings from house to house, these are mom-made groups of friends and neighbors with kids the same age.

   Pros: These groups are generally made up of your friends who presumably get along. You'll get the inside scoop on all sorts of local information, including preschool evaluations and town events. Everyone gets out of the house, and they share more than just toys: moms with bigger kids pass down clothes, bike helmets, and so on, not to mention maternity clothes, electronic breast pumps (note: buy fresh tubing), and such, thereby saving you money.

Cons: Eventually, all those toddlers and their moms will be at your house. You have to RSVP your regrets, and you'll probably feel guilty if you don't attend simply because you don't feel like going out in the cold today. Mom-made playgroups are not immune to politics, and you have to monitor your toddler's every move, in case he gets into your neighbor's good china or decides to wallop Jacob for touching his toy.

> "Playdates are best kept short at this age. As awesome as it is to socialize with the other moms, the kids just have a hard time holding it together for too long and things get crazy."
>
> —*Julie, West Chester, Pennsylvania*

It worked for me!

WE ASKED: What's the worst part about toddlers?

"Discipline. They seem so little, yet they know exactly what they are doing."

—*Crystal, San Antonio, Texas*

Do You Need to Entertain Your Playgroup?

There are three schools of thought when it comes to supervising toddler play:

1. The moms need to plan and organize every gathering, like an entertainment director on a cruise ship.

2. The moms need to monitor play so that nobody gets hurt and divert attention in case the fun runs out and everybody's in a tizzy.

3. The moms need a drink.

I follow the philosophy of group number two, though I have been known to organize a soccer game in the backyard or a lemonade stand in the driveway, but never on the same day.

When I wanted my toddlers to have some structured play, I signed them up for Playorama classes so that somebody else could sing the "Hello" song and blow bubbles. I don't want to sing the "Hello" song. I want to sit on the sidelines and watch my toddlers ignore the lady singing the "Hello" song, while they climb through the big blue tunnel before they're supposed to, and I sigh.

If you have a desire to plan out activities such as these for your playgroup, you probably don't need me to tell you how. But if you've never been to such an event, here's pretty much how it goes:

The moms, dads, grandparents, and nannies enter the meeting room or house with their toddlers and take off jackets, snowsuits, shoes, and so on. Somebody winds up needing a diaper change, which they protest vehemently because, darn it, there are toys to play with, and they don't have time for this nonsense.

One toddler clings to her mother's pants while Mommy implores her to go play. Many toddlers gather around the teacher, who sings and "kisses" each toddler with a teddy bear. A few others (mine, probably) put big foam blocks into the playhouse before they run circles around everyone else.

The "leader" invites all the kids to sit in a circle and sing such standards as "Head and Shoulders, Knees and Toes." Some of the kids do it. Others (mine, probably) go about their own business. Then the leader sets up an obstacle course for the kids to play on.

Moms (mostly) try to maintain conversations while following their toddlers around the room, helping them get in and out of the rubber tires and down the slide without bonking their heads. Somebody needs a diaper change or a trip to the potty, which they protest. Somebody else fights over a toy, and that one kid still clings to her mother's pants.

The leader asks everyone to help clear out the matted area, and then the kids sit on top of the parachute while the moms grab the ends and pull their toddlers in a circle. Even the mom with a baby in a sling lugs the toddler-laden parachute. Then the kids go under the parachute while the moms lift it up and down while singing something that you won't hear on a classic rock radio station.

The moms get a little break while the leader puts the parachute away and gets out the bubbles, which is like the part of the concert when the audience holds up their lighters: nobody wants it to end. Then the kids who want stamps on their hands get one in preparation, perhaps, for future clubbing. Then everyone packs up and leaves, except the kids who need diaper changes.

If you want to organize all that, go ahead. I'd much prefer to let someone else do it, or for playdates and playgroups at home, just let the kids play with the toys while the moms shove muffins down their throats and sit for just a moment.

Whether your toddler has a playdate or a playgroup, keep in mind that such gatherings are as much for you as they are for your toddler. You need a break from the one-on-one (or one-on-more-than-one), so make sure that however you set up your toddler's social calendar, it works for you, too

> **It worked for me!**
>
> "I have made some of my best mommy friends via play groups. Find a local MOPS group or small group at church. Go to Gymboree or MyGym or something like that. Be open, but not desperate!"
>
> —*Chrissy, Dillsburg, Pennsylvania*

Gimme a break

Join Your Own Playgroup

Whether it's a tennis team, a scrap-booking group, or a bowling league, join or create your own playgroup that meets sans kids. Mommy should get to play, too!

Just a Minute!

BETWEEN THE LINES: THE PLAYGROUP INVITATION

Greater Somerset Playgroup for Like-Minded Moms—All Are Welcome!!

(If you don't have a Bugaboo stroller, you are not like-minded.)

We are a playgroup for moms of toddlers
in the greater Somerset area.

*(And, unlike those moms from the other Somerset Area Playgroup,
we don't bad-mouth when someone lets their kid
watch a little TV now and then.)*

We have weekly gatherings at parks,
playgrounds, and other fun places.

*(You know, instead of trashing each other's houses
with organic yogurt and flaxseed, whatever the hell that is.)*

We also have potluck lunches and a monthly Moms' Night Out!!!

(Because after thirty days of whine, who doesn't need some wine?)

Great socialization for your toddler.

*(And for Mommy, who needs to stop ordering things online
just so she can talk to the UPS guy.)*

If you're looking for a safe place to make new friends, join us!

(If you bake, we love you already.)

Call Jenn 555-1234.

(But NEVER during nap time.)

READER/CUSTOMER CARE SURVEY

We care about your opinions! Please take a moment to fill out our online Reader Survey at **http://survey.hcibooks.com.**
As a **"THANK YOU"** you will receive a **VALUABLE INSTANT COUPON** towards future book purchases
as well as a **SPECIAL GIFT** available only online! Or, you may mail this card back to us.

(PLEASE PRINT IN ALL CAPS)

First Name		MI.	Last Name

Address			City

State	Zip	Email	

1. Gender
- ☐ Female ☐ Male

2. Age
- ☐ 8 or younger
- ☐ 9-12 ☐ 13-16
- ☐ 17-20 ☐ 21-30
- ☐ 31+

3. Did you receive this book as a gift?
- ☐ Yes ☐ No

4. Annual Household Income
- ☐ under $25,000
- ☐ $25,000 - $34,999
- ☐ $35,000 - $49,999
- ☐ $50,000 - $74,999
- ☐ over $75,000

5. What are the ages of the children living in your house?
- ☐ 0 - 14 ☐ 15+

6. Marital Status
- ☐ Single
- ☐ Married
- ☐ Divorced
- ☐ Widowed

7. How did you find out about the book?
(please choose one)
- ☐ Recommendation
- ☐ Store Display
- ☐ Online
- ☐ Catalog/Mailing
- ☐ Interview/Review

8. Where do you usually buy books?
(please choose one)
- ☐ Bookstore
- ☐ Online
- ☐ Book Club/Mail Order
- ☐ Price Club (Sam's Club, Costco's, etc.)
- ☐ Retail Store (Target, Wal-Mart, etc.)

9. What subject do you enjoy reading about the most?
(please choose one)
- ☐ Parenting/Family
- ☐ Relationships
- ☐ Recovery/Addictions
- ☐ Health/Nutrition
- ☐ Christianity
- ☐ Spirituality/Inspiration
- ☐ Business Self-help
- ☐ Women's Issues
- ☐ Sports

10. What attracts you most to a book?
(please choose one)
- ☐ Title
- ☐ Cover Design
- ☐ Author
- ☐ Content

FOLD HERE

Comments

Chapter Eight

Who Is This Kid and Why Is He Calling Me "Mommy"?
Discipline and Dealing with the Unpredictable Nature of Toddlers

WE ASKED: What surprised you most about the toddler stage?

"The nanosecond it takes to go from cool to chaos."

—*Julie, West Chester, Pennsylvania*

One morning, my sister-in-law found a Tonka truck in her refrigerator. This surprised her as her daughter had never thought to stock toys in the appliances. Her eighteen-month-old son, however, thought this made perfect sense. And it made sense to me, too, because I'd seen it before.

I had two toddlers who felt the need to relocate various household items, their toys, my books, our shoes, and so on. Over the years, I've found plastic dinosaurs in my plants and red foam rubber balls in my tissue box. (What? No rabbit?) One day, I drove twenty miles wondering what the strange noise in the back of my minivan was before I discovered that it was a Spiderman glove with "real web-making sounds"! I've found crackers in my shoes, stickers in the dryer, and Matchbox cars in my pockets. Thanks to my toddlers, every day was like a surprise party, and I was the guest of honor. Surprise, Mommy! There's a red and yellow plastic hammer in the utensil drawer!

Toddlers are an unpredictable lot. They can go from sweet to sour (and supercranky) in no time flat. One second they love grilled cheese, and the next it's hot dogs or nothing, Mommy! Your toddler is finding herself (and her true personality) in the midst of all the ups and downs, while you're finding all sorts of things in odd places. How do you keep life with your toddler as even-keeled as possible, even when there's a Tonka truck in the crisper?

Okay, I admit it. . . .

"Last night I was on the phone. When I got off and realized that I had an actual conversation without my toddler trying to grab at the phone, I got a bit nervous. I looked behind the island in the kitchen, and somehow he had gotten to the maple syrup bottle. He proceeded to dump almost the entire bottle on himself and on the floor. It was almost like a scene out of a Tim Conway skit. Every time he tried to get up, he'd slip and fall.

—*Lisa,*
Blue Bell, Pennsylvania

Looking for Trouble in All the Wrong Places

LIVING WITH A toddler is like being in a biker bar late on a Saturday night: you never know when all hell will break loose. Your toddler may go from quietly playing with a toy on the living room floor one minute to attempting to break into your media cabinet the next. If only you could hire 24/7 video surveillance for your tot. Maybe then you could cook dinner without putting the wooden spoon down every two minutes to spot-check your kid.

Just like in sports, the best offense is a good defense when it comes to parenting a toddler. In other words, you're gonna have to keep a really close eye on your one- to three-year-old until she becomes more predictable and less interested in the (open-close-open-close-open- . . .) DVD player. You can rely on childproofing only so much. My toddlers unlatched those toilet-proofers faster than Houdini could escape a straitjacket. I should have just flushed $7.99 down the toilet and saved myself the trouble.

But take heart: there's a reason mothers have eyes in the backs of their heads. Use those eyes and trust your gut when it tells you it's too quiet wherever your toddler is right now. In the meantime, consider five of the most common behaviors of toddlers looking for trouble, along with tips on how to deal with them—or avoid them altogether.

Five Common Toddler Troubles

1. **Touches what he shouldn't.** He's got a toy box that could fill Santa's sleigh, and yet, the buttons on the TV are way more

fun to play with and turn on . . . and turn off . . . turn on . . . push the VOLUME BUTTON ALL THE WAY UP until the neighbors can hear the five-day weather forecast and a commercial for 1-800 Mattress while you scramble for the remote and your composure. What can you do?

Think like a toddler: When your toddler is asleep, get down to toddler eye level and think like him, or, perhaps, like drunken college kids on the prowl—the outcome is similar. Assuming you've done the major childproofing in the house (see Chapter 5 for details), you're looking for the things they don't sell childproofing gadgets for. Now is the time to store the valuable stuff in a closet and put things you use regularly, such as the TV's remote control and the tissue box, high out of reach. Unplug the TV and latch or even duct tape your media hutch shut if you don't want to broadcast the evening news to the neighbors.

Just say "No": This is a great time to start teaching your toddler some discipline. If he's got a fetish for the fireplace doors, grab his hand when he goes for them and say firmly, but without a lot of emotion, "No." Keep this up, even if you have to do it a few dozen times a day. If it's not okay to touch the fireplace doors on Tuesday, it's not okay on Wednesday. If you let him play with them once because you're busy making dinner, he won't understand that they are off limits, and he'll touch them a few more dozen times every day until he breaks something or loses interest— or you lose your mind.

2. **Throws or dumps food.** If your toddler acts like John Belushi in *Animal House* starting a food fight at every meal, you're not alone. Toddlers love to make messes, especially when they're bored with sitting for so long. What can you do?

Ditch dinner fast: As soon as the first hot dog zooms past your face, pull your toddler out of her high chair and say "No throwing." Experts will tell you to distract your toddler by setting up a creative activity. Phooey. All you're teaching her is, "If you're bored with dinner, just chuck a roll at Mommy's face and she'll play with your dollhouse with you!" Send your toddler the message: You throw, you don't eat it, and dinner's not over.

Dole it slowly: Ah, but what if you've got a picky eater who soon learns that throwing food equals losing the yucky peas real fast? Don't put the entire meal in front of him at once. Instead, keep your toddler's food out of his reach and feed him yourself. He can learn how to use the spoon when he's past his stage of chucking it across the room.

3. **Freaks out easily.** Does your toddler switch from easygoing to going postal in a seemingly short amount of time? If it's like living with a miniature version of Tony Soprano, you're going to have to learn how to manage your toddler's temper without letting it rule the house.

Predict and diffuse: If you know your toddler is going to have a canary because his cousin just touched his favorite Elmo doll, swoop in and distract him with something better, like a new and, therefore, more attractive toy, a snack, or when all else fails—dare I say—a video. Or prevent the whole thing in the first place by hiding Elmo from everyone.

Let it rip: Sometimes your toddler just has to get it out of her system. Let her scream it out—all alone—somewhere where she can't hurt herself or Aunt Mary's collection of Hummels. Chances are she won't like being alone for too long. When she dials it down, let her come back. But if she starts up again, isolate her and her wails again.

4. **Has trouble focusing.** You left the playgroup fifteen minutes ago, and yet you still haven't reached your car. Between the door and the parking lot, you have now stopped nine times to look at a caterpillar, some pretty flowers, another caterpillar, a birdie, birdie poop, a bubble gum wrapper, and look! A leaf! While it's hardly fascinating enough for you to warrant such interest, your toddler can't help himself. No matter how many times you remind him, "It's time to go now, Dillon," he can't focus on leaving or, apparently, on any one thing. Hey! It's a worm!

   Make firm announcements: You can say "We're going to be late" a bazillion times to a toddler, but it means little to him. First of all, he has no concept of time, or they'd make wristwatches in 2T. Second, he's just got to check things out, because being a toddler is like landing on the moon for the first time: everything is exciting and new. He just might want to bring that rock back for further research. But if you say, "Look at one more leaf, and then we're going to the car," he might understand better, especially if you actually go to the car after one more leaf. If you don't do what you say you're going to do, your announcements are as useless as empty campaign promises after the inauguration.

Use the power of distraction: If you know that your toddler will want to stop to investigate that puddle ahead, but you're in a hurry, don't let her see it. Scoop her up and focus on how wonderfully amazing the twig she just picked up is until you bypass the puddle and make it to the car, the store, the house, day care, wherever.

5. **Wears all the wrong clothes.** Some toddlers like to pick out their own clothes, leaving you to wish there was a *What Not to Wear* intervention for toddlers. You put out a nice jumper and tights for a birthday party today, but your toddler insists on wearing her Scooby Doo pj's over the leopard-print pants your sister-in-law gave her for Hanukkah. Oh, and snow boots—in May. Before you call in the fashion experts, try these tactics.

   Limit outfit options: Teach your toddler that she doesn't have carte blanche when it comes to selecting an outfit. Put out two or three outfits at most and let her choose one. Make sure they're interchangeable, in case she decides to wear the top from one outfit and the pants from another.

   Choose your battles: Does it really matter if your toddler dresses in his Tigger Halloween costume when you go for a walk with your neighbor? As long as he's not too hot or too cold, give in on some of his wardrobe choices to keep the peace. He'll feel like he's independent and grown-up, and you'll be relieved to avoid another battle.

WE ASKED: What do you wish someone had told you about parenting toddlers before you had them?

"That you will not get as much done as you had hoped."

—*Holly, Britt, Iowa*

Antisocialites, Crazy-Makers, and More

I THOUGHT I'D finally gotten him to fall asleep. My toddler was lying in my bed next to me, holding his favorite vacuum attachment (don't ask), apparently sleeping. Just when I thought it was safe to doze off, he lifted his head, looked me in the eye, and furrowed his brow as though he was about to tell me something very important.

"D," he said before putting his head back down.

I have no idea what "D" meant, except perhaps, "I'm not going to let you sleep tonight."

Toddlers.

Okay, I admit it. . . .

"I wish someone had told me that it's like having an unmedicated schizophrenic suicidal know-it-all without bladder control, on uppers 24/7."

—*Colleen, Tucson, Arizona*

You can tell yourself that your toddler's crazy behaviors are part of her "exploration of her world" and her quest for "asserting her independence" and all that other parenting expert mumbo jumbo. But when your toddler is refusing to wear her socks in thirty-degree weather, all that world exploring and independence asserting don't help you get to church on time.

Your toddler will no doubt come up with some crazy behaviors that may confound you, annoy you, or even amuse you. How you deal with them will determine how easy or how hard the toddler years will be on you. Here are a few of the most common crazy-making behaviors your toddler might make.

Refuses to Wear Socks, Coats, Hats . . .

Not to be confused with the Naked Newbie (see Chapter 2), this kid has an issue with specific items of clothing. He's the toddler who might refuse to wear socks or shoes. It works for him just fine in the summer, but try to put something on his feet when the forecast is for flurries, and you'll likely get one big foot-fit all the way to the snowdrifts. What can you do?

Don't try to reason with him. Your toddler doesn't care why you want him to wear proper footwear. He just knows it feels good to run barefoot through the mall while you frantically chase him right up to the Cinnabon counter.

Do make new rules. No shoes inside houses is okay with you. If nothing else, your child will have a great future doing business in Japan. But stick to your guns when it comes to wearing shoes in foul weather, public places, and for your Christmas card photo. As long as your toddler knows he'll get to run barefoot part of the time, he'll learn to compromise the rest of the time—eventually.

> **It worked for me!**
>
> "Some toddlers have to carry a blanket or stuffed animal with them everywhere they go. Not my two-and-a-half-year-old daughter, Julia. Her favorite objects to carry are a couple of bookmarks or business cards—one for each hand. Of course she ends up dropping them when we're out and then insists that I keep picking them up.
>
> "Eventually, I tell her if she drops her paper one more time we're leaving it. So she's left her trail of bookmarks in stores all over the place. Of course, I guess bookmarks are better than when she was in her phase of carrying two clothes hangers everywhere."
>
> —Francine, Annandale, New Jersey

Nope, She's Not Listening to You

You know she can hear you. She's just pretending that you're not telling her it's time for bed, because she'd much rather continue hosting a tea party with her Cabbage Patch dolls. So she ignores you. After all, you ignore her when you're trying to read the newspaper, and she says, "Mommy. Mommy. Mommy. Mommy. Mommy. Mommy." So now what?

Don't nag. It doesn't work on your husband when you say, "Could you just once get your underpants into the hamper, or do

I have to do everything around here?" And it won't work on your toddler, who thinks that you really should do everything around here.

Do give her very specific directions without asking questions. In other words, "Come into the bathroom now" works much better than "Can you stop playing, honey?" Because the answer to the latter question is a big fat "No." Also, be consistent. You can't tell her to come into the bathroom now and then get on the phone for ten minutes. *Now* means *now* all the time, or she's not going to take your orders seriously.

Head Butts Like a Ram During Mating Season

You tell your toddler it's time to leave the playground, but he wants none of it. Instead of throwing a temper tantrum or biting you, he hauls off and butts his head into your nose. Ouch! Toddlers usually butt heads for one of two reasons: (1) they aren't able to verbalize their discontent, or (2) they think it's fun, like a tickle fit. Short of wearing a mouth guard and face mask for a few months, what can you do?

Don't laugh. He may look particularly funny as he winds up like a cartoon bull and races toward you, but laughing only encourages him. And eventually, he's going to go headfirst into your face. Besides, he's head level with your husband's privates. Do everyone a favor and nip the head butting right away.

Do help him find the words he can't say yet. If he doesn't want to leave the playground, look him in the eye and say, "No head butting! You're sad because you don't want to leave, right?" And then let him have a few more minutes to play, but make sure he understands you're leaving after he gets twenty more swings or five more runs down the slide, or he'll just butt heads again when it's time to go.

WE ASKED: What are your favorite ways to keep your toddler busy when you need some time for yourself (or to fold laundry in peace)?

"Giving them a full pack of sticky notes and letting them tear off one sheet at a time. I also used to put my daughter in her high chair and fill the tray with a little bit of water and let her go crazy."

—*Lisa, Blue Bell, Pennsylvania*

Asks the Same Thing Over and Over and Over and Over . . .

You're just trying to make it through Hallmark, so you can buy a few birthday cards and some wrapping paper, but your toddler keeps stopping and asking, "What dat?" You answer, "Bows. Those are pretty bows." And then, as though you hadn't just had a conversation about the damn bows, she asks, "What dat?" while pointing at the very same bows. Argh! What dat? Dat's annoying, that's what dat. How can you make it through your long day with what appears to be the world's most amnesiac child?

Don't shout, "Those are bows, just like I told you thirty seconds ago!" no matter how good it might feel. Sometimes toddlers are less interested in the answer than they are in the question. "What dat?" can be more about showing off her ability to speak in a sentence and hear you respond than it is finding out what dat is. Or she could be trying to learn new words. Think about it: did you remember that "lapiz" is the word for "pencil" when you first heard it in Spanish class? Or did you have to ask, "¿Qué es eso?" a few times before you learned it?

Do summon up as much patience as humanly possible and answer her questions. Yes, that means you have to answer the very same question thirty times. If you're having one of those days where her incessant questions feel like they're burning holes in your brain, initiate No Question Zones, where, for example, she's not allowed to ask you "What dat?" through all of Hallmark. Or get her one of those board books where you push the button and it says a word. I recommend that you put some duct tape over the speaker, because those things have no volume control and there isn't enough Excedrin to get you through a speed round of farm animal names as described by Elmo.

WE ASKED: What surprised you most about the toddler stage?

"How much I love it and hate it at the same time."

—Kelly, Wickliffe, Ohio

Sucks His Thumb

This is only really a problem in one of two situations: (1) his thumb sucking is making his front teeth protrude, and (2) it bothers you. Ask yourself, is it really a problem? Chances are he won't suck his thumb in algebra class some day. Eventually, he'll stop doing it. But if you want to help him quit the habit now, here's what to do.

Don't worry too much. Most kids quit sucking their thumbs before their permanent teeth come in. In fact, the vast majority quit before they're five. Also, don't keep pulling his thumb out of his mouth, or you'll just make it all that more appealing to him.

Do praise your toddler for refraining from sucking his thumb. The American Dental Association recommends bandaging your toddler's thumb or applying a bitter tasting medication your pediatrician can prescribe. Or use vinegar. But that's for kids over age four. Really, at this age, you shouldn't worry too much about a toddler who sucks his thumb.

Whiiiiiiiiiiiines

Your toddler wants you to play with her right now, but you're busy making dinner. So she stands behind you whiiiiiiining until you cave in, turn off the burner, and go play with her.

Sucker.

Whining is your toddler's way of manipulating you into doing what she wants you to do. If you let her get away with it now because she's "just a baby," picture yourself at the mall in ten years trying to explain to your whining tween why she can't have a skin-tight T-shirt that reads: "Is it hot in here or is it me?" If you don't quash the whining now, you'll be looking at years of it ahead of you because your toddler will know it works, and works well. How do you get your toddler to stop whining?

Don't yell at her to "quit whining, wouldya?" Getting a rise out of you is part of the fun, fun, fun of whining in the first place. Ignore your toddler's whining, no matter how much it rattles your nerves like a squeaky door to the kitchen of a busy restaurant. Ignore it, and you'll teach her that whining has no effect on you.

Do be consistent when you say "no" because, though toddlers often have short-term memories, they will remember that one time you said "yes" and not the nineteen other times you said "no." And it will be worth it to them to whine, whine, whine their way to another "yes," even if it takes another nineteen times until they get it.

Momma Said   **WE ASKED:** How can you get your toddler to behave better?

"*Ignore her!* That's always been the worst thing for my daughter, because she hates to be ignored more than anything. As long as she's safe and not going to really hurt herself, I'd just walk away or pick up a magazine or something to show I wasn't paying attention."

—*Rebecca, Bluff City, Tennessee*

Talks Back

You think you're simply offering your toddler some corn, but she holds up her hand, makes a face as though she's just smelled the Lincoln Tunnel during a traffic jam, and shouts, "No! Yucky!"

Your toddler is showing some 'tude, and you're not liking it. But before you send her to her room without dinner, remember she's not quite old enough to be thinking, *I'll show you who's boss around here.* Rather, she probably just doesn't want corn. How do you stop the sass before it becomes a habit?

> **Okay, I admit it. • • •**
>
> "I hate trying to get mascara off the wall—and lipstick, and lotion—and the fact that I thought she was asleep when she was really becoming an artist!"
>
> —*Shelley, Travis AFB, California*

Don't yell, "Don't talk to me that way, young lady!" She doesn't understand what you mean any more than she'd grasp a long lesson on manners.

Do teach her a better way to voice her discontent. Tell her, "Say 'no thank you,'" and then praise her when she does. If she uses a word that's verboten in your house, tell her she can't say it. "We don't say yucky" or stinky or poopy or whatever gets the point across to a toddler who hates your yucky corn.

Gets into Everything

Just when you thought you had a moment to yourself to shave both legs on the same day or read the mail, you discover that your toddler has gotten into yet another fine mess—this time, the eggs, which are now all over your kitchen floor. You feel like you're caught in a *Dennis the Menace* episode, only you're not laughing.

Why do toddlers get into anything and everything they find? Because they can, that's why. But short of wiring your entire house with motion detector alarms, what can you do?

Don't frantically dash from mess to mess, shouting, "I just cleaned up in here!" Your toddler doesn't care. All he cares about is that you're ruining his masterpiece by cleaning up the eggs. Don't forget to give your toddler his own space to make a mess. For example, plop him down on a huge piece of brown wrapping paper and give him crayons and free will, or at least twenty minutes to make a complete, yet controlled, mess.

Do get right up in his face and say firmly, "No! Don't touch the eggs!" or whatever mess he's made before you clean it up. He needs to understand that he's done something bad. The more serious the infraction (such as breaking good plates on purpose or throwing your car keys into the lake), the more serious the reaction. Take away his favorite lovey for a while or place him in a short time-out, though remember that kids under two generally don't understand the time-out concept. Still, removing him from the crime scene is a good idea. Finally, do some creative toddler-proofing (see Chapter 5) to prevent your toddler from getting into everything in the first place.

> "If a fit ensues, I tell her to let me know when she is done. She comes up afterward and says, 'Momma, I'm done,' and she gets a hug."
>
> —Julie, West Chester, Pennsylvania

It worked for me!

She Loves You, She Loves You Not

Some days, your toddler has more mood swings than Faye Dunaway in *Mommie Dearest*. If you wait long enough, your toddler just might shout, "No wire hangers!" at you. At least it can feel that way. The terrible truth is that the Terrible Twos start early and last a long, long time. What can you do when your toddler adores you one minute and abhors you the next?

Don't kid yourself. Your toddler is the center of her own little universe no matter how many manners and rules you think she's learned. When you disturb her universe, she's going to let you know it. Understand that your toddler's mood can change faster than the winds atop Mount Everest. Be prepared for foul weather, and you'll endure the Terrible Twos.

Do try to identify the triggers of your toddler's outbursts. If she gets easily frustrated with new tasks, don't let her attempt them when she's particularly tired and cranky, because it'll only make her mood swing even further. Try to validate her feelings. Say, "You're angry because you can't get the block into the box." Who doesn't want someone else to understand their feelings? Take advantage of her short attention span. Divert her attention from the thing that's driving her mad to something else, and her mood will calm down considerably.

WE ASKED: What surprised you the most about the toddler stage?

"The unsolicited affection. I have endless examples, but my favorite moment was when I was on my hands and knees cleaning the kitchen floor, and my daughter came up to me. She called my name, held my chin in one hand, used her other hand to lift my bangs, and then planted the most wonderful kiss on my forehead. After the kiss, she put both hands on each of my cheeks and looked me straight in the face and told me she loved me. Then she quickly ran off to keep playing whatever she was playing."

—*Trisha, West Chester, Pennsylvania*

"Remember, we were all two."

—*Barb, Denver, Colorado*

It worked for me!

Gimme a break

Mommy Needs a Time-Out

If you find yourself increasingly frustrated and angry at your toddler's antics, take a time-out. Put your toddler in his room while you go scream in a pillow. Leave your toddler with a neighbor or your husband so you can go for a long, head-clearing walk, or turn on the TV for your toddler so you can go cool down.

Just a minute!

Wheel of Toddlers

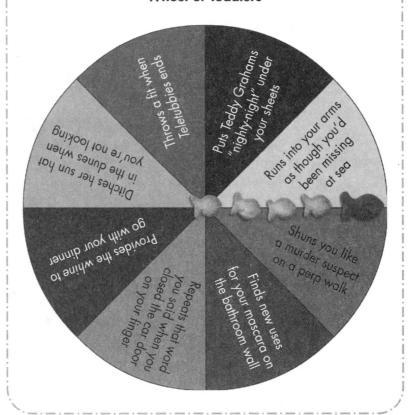

- Puts Teddy Grahams "nighty-night" under your sheets
- Runs into your arms as though you'd been missing at sea
- Shuns you like a murder suspect on a perp walk
- Finds new uses for your mascara on the bathroom wall
- Repeats that word you said when you closed the car door on your finger
- Provides the whine to go with your dinner
- Ditches her sun hat in the dunes when you're not looking
- Throws a fit when Teletubbies ends

Chapter Nine

Beyond *Blue's Clues:*
Entertaining Your Toddler

> "I gave him things that weren't his toys—stuff from the kitchen, brooms, my books or magazines, etc."
>
> —*Kelly, Wickliffe, Ohio*

It worked for me!

For several winters, it felt like I didn't go anywhere. First, there was the winter after my second son was born, when I spent my days pat-pat-patting my colicky newborn's back while trying to keep my twenty-month-old entertained and away from the pantry and the remote control for the TV. Then there was the winter I potty trained my first son and it felt like we spent months watching *It's Potty Time* while I tried to keep my fourteen-month-old away from the pantry and the remote control for the TV. Then there was the winter everybody caught the flu over and over again.

As a result, I became very adept at entertaining toddlers, even in less-than-ideal situations, like when Nicholas had the stomach flu and Mommy had morning sickness. Let's just say it was like a frat house on a Sunday morning. Yet I managed to keep us both busy nonetheless.

As a full-time stay-at-home mom, I learned how to fill upwards of 100 hours a week, some of it with entertaining and even educational activities, yet some of it with letting my toddlers pull all of the tissues out of the box and then stuff them back in. Did I mention it was *100 hours a week*?

So, how do you keep your toddlers entertained, whether it's for one hour or an entire week? Here's the inside scoop.

WE ASKED: What are your favorite ways to keep your toddler busy?

"Having her 'cook' for me in her kitchen."

—*Leandra, Sumter, South Carolina*

Why Do Toddlers Play?

PLAY IS MORE than a way to fill the hours. Play is how toddlers develop their fine and gross motor skills, figure out how things work, learn language, work through emotions, and exercise. And it's not just about toys, either. They learn from all sorts of play.

My eighteen-month-old nephew is currently in his "swapsies" stage: he hands you a toy and then swaps it for another before swapping it back. To him, this is as much fun as mah-jongg is to the ladies down at the JCC. When he had ten people to play swapsies with at a recent family gathering, he was as excited as a contestant with thirty cases to open on *Deal or No Deal.* Oh, the possibilities!

With toddlers, play is simple. That's why you really don't need to stock your house with a lot of educational toys. They might make you feel better when you leave your toddler to play while you check your e-mail, but your toddler really is learning something simply by stacking the plastic cups up and taking them apart over and over again. Toddlers learn through play, and play doesn't necessarily have to involve the alphabet or numbers to teach them something valuable.

Four Fun Activities Toddlers Love

1. **Clean up.** Hand your toddler toys to put away—one by one—into the toy box. When your toddler goes through the happy-to-clean-up stage, this activity not only keeps them busy, it keeps the family room clean, too. You can also try putting trading cards into a box, balls into a bag, blocks into their container, and so on.

2. **Cheerios trail.** Set a trail of Cheerios along the coffee table. Let your toddler eat them one by one. If you're lucky, you'll

get to sit on the couch and watch the weather report while your toddler heads down the Cheerio trail.

3. **Cabinet hideaway.** Empty out a kitchen cabinet and let your toddler climb in. Supply Tupperware, pots, or even toys. It's a perfect activity for when you're cooking and need to keep an eye on your toddler. Hang a dishtowel over the cabinet door to keep it from closing on your toddler.

4. **Fridge fun.** Pull the magnets off the refrigerator. Put them back on. Repeat. Just make sure none of them are small enough to be choking hazards.

Toys for Toddlers

What should you buy your toddler? (Or better yet, what should Grandma buy?) Toddlers love cause-and-effect toys: they do something and something happens. These include:

- Shape sorters
- Pop-up toys
- Toys with things they make move, talk, and so on (You know, "The cow says 'moo.'")
- Balls
- Building blocks
- Musical toys (You might take these in small doses, Mom.)

They also love anything that lets them move:

- Push and pull toys
- Ride-on toys
- Tricycles (ages two years and up)
- Toy vacuums, mowers, shopping carts

Toddlers love toys that repeat. Toddlers love toys that repeat. Toddlers love . . . :

- Anything where you push a button and the toy makes noise, sings a song, or pops up
- Sandboxes (Fill the bucket. Empty the bucket. Repeat.)
- Toy trucks/cars

Toddlers love to imitate. They like toy versions of grown-up things, such as:

- Cell phones, phones, cameras
- Tea sets, dishes, pots, and pans
- Gardening and workshop tools
- Babies (dolls, that is)
- Car keys
- Steering wheels
- Musical instruments

Toddlers love stuff that lets them be creative, even if you're not exactly sure what they've made:

- Crayons, washable markers, paper
- Play-Doh, clay
- Finger paints (You really have to supervise this closely, or you'll end up with paint everywhere.)
- Bathtub paints and markers
- Driveway chalk
- Etch-A-Sketch

Other fun stuff:

- Large-piece puzzles
- Dress-up clothes, costumes
- Board books
- Playground sets, swings
- Floating toys for the tub or kiddie pool

There are a few educational toys worth buying for your toddler, but the hottest toys change so often, I can't list them all in a book. To find out the best educational toys for your toddler, visit independent toy reviewers, such as Dr. Toy.com (http://drtoy.com) or Consumer Reports (http://www.consumersreport.org), for the latest and greatest.

"Pull out secret weapon toys. I keep a box of toys that will be new when I pull them out and then put them back away for a necessary time. They are new all over again."

It worked for me!

—*Crystal, San Antonio, Texas*

Momma Said

WE ASKED: What are your favorite ways to keep your toddler busy?

"We're big on stickers. Makes you have to fold the laundry in the kitchen to make sure the stickers don't end up stuck on the cabinets, but it's worth it."

—*Susan, Montville, New Jersey*

Twelve Things to Do When You're Trapped in the House

1. **Traffic jam.** Line up all of your toddler's bazillion toy cars in a big, snaking traffic jam throughout a room in your house. If your toddler is old enough, teach him to make patterns—all red cars, then blue ones, or all trucks and then all cars, and so on.

2. **Beauty school dropout.** Offer manicures and pedicures. Or let your toddler style your hair.

3. **Bear tea party.** Invite your toddler's favorite stuffed animals for a tea party in the dining room. (It may be the only time

you actually use the dining room other than Thanksgiving dinner.)

4. **Dino archaeologist.** Let your toddler make imprints of her plastic dinosaurs' feet (or face, or whatever) in Play-Doh.

5. **Tupperware party.** Surround your toddler with Tupperware or other unbreakable plastic ware. Give her two wooden spoons. Put on music and let her drum like Ringo. Suggestion: Get out the earplugs before you dole out the spoons.

6. **Toddler ink.** Tape several temporary tattoos onto a piece of cardboard, or hang them with magnets on the fridge. Let your toddler choose which tattoo(s) he'd like to get.

7. **Toy box bonanza.** Clean out your toy box. You'll be surprised at the treasures under the T.M.X. Elmo and all those blocks. It's like getting new toys, which, of course, will entertain your toddler for quite some time. (Similarly, yesterday's Pop-Tarts are today's science project. Make sure you supervise the clean-out, in case you find something green that shouldn't be.)

8. **Midday bath.** Relax by the bathtub while your toddler plays in a rare midday bath. Give her bath paints and plastic goodies to play with. Call it a swim, and let her wear her swim goggles and swimmies.

9. **The morning story.** Why wait until bedtime for a story? Snack time is a great time for a story. If nothing else, it'll keep your toddler in one place for a little while.

10. **Sink it.** Fill a bowl with water and place it in the kitchen sink. Pull up a stool or small chair and let your toddler play with the turkey baster, spoons, sifter, and whatever else (safely) entertains him. You can use food coloring to turn the water different colors. But please, always supervise your toddler around water.

11. **Box lunch.** If you have a delivery of large appliances or furniture, ask the delivery person to leave behind the box. Using paints or markers, turn it into a spaceship or a restaurant that serves PB&J sandwiches.

12. **Indoor picnic.** Spread out a blanket on the living room or kitchen floor. Pack lunch or snacks in a basket and pretend to have a picnic indoors.

It worked for me!

"Some people say that they don't want to waste time or money on doing [special activities] with their toddlers because they won't remember it, but I think that is rubbish! It does not matter if they remember it, because it is still beneficial to their brain development, their language development, and their cognitive development."

—Emily, Katy, Texas

> "Keep a favorite DVD fresher by not playing it much."
>
> —*Kellie, Derby, Connecticut*

It worked for me!

Ten Things to Do Away from Home

1. **Little errands.** Need to get out of the house, but have nowhere to go? Tell your toddler you need her help. Her job? She's in charge of pulling all the mail out of your post office box or filling a shopping basket with plates, cups, and party favors, or handing rolls of coins one-by-one (if there's no line behind you, of course) to the cashier at the bank. If you're lucky, you'll kill an hour while tiring your toddler out. Better yet, you'll teach her to help you when you're out and about.

2. **All aboard.** Take your toddler to watch the trains come and go at the train station—likewise for planes at a small airport or boats at a marina.

3. **There goes a bulldozer.** Take your kids to watch construction trucks. If your neighbor is doing renovations or the town is working on the road out front, you don't have far to go. My sons and I watched a Home Depot being built. One rainy day, we watched the cement mixer spin and spin for an hour. (Bring a magazine, in case you're not as interested in backhoes as your toddler is.)

4. **My little pony.** If you have horse stables nearby, take your toddler to watch the horses run. Just make sure the stable owners don't mind you hanging around. They might even let you bring carrots to feed the horses.

5. **By the sea.** The ocean is fun to visit in the off-season, when your toddler can chase down the seagulls without running through anyone's beach blanket. Same goes for the boardwalk.

6. **Making pies.** Visit the bagel shop or pizzeria to watch food as it's being made.

7. **Pet shop boys (or girls).** Go see the bunnies, puppies, kittens, and birds at the pet shop. Let your kids pick out a new tag for your pet, if you have one. Many pet stores have automatic tag makers that are fun to watch.

8. **School's out.** Watch the school buses leaving the local school in the afternoon. The bigger the school, the more buses to watch.

9. **The gardens.** Take your toddler to walk through lines of colorful flowers at an outdoor garden store. He'll love the fountains and the flags for sale, too.

10. **Pick a cookie.** After all that on-the-go activity, you deserve a cookie. Drop by the bakery to peer through the cases and pick out cookies for both of you.

Five Things to Do in the Yard

1. **Rock out.** Collect small rocks in a bucket. You can even make a rock garden, where your toddler dumps rocks and pebbles. It's something for her to work on every day. You might even be able to get some gardening done while she's busy.

2. **Worm hunt.** Dig up worms. Toddlers love to watch them. Or check puddles after a rainstorm where you'll likely see more worms than you ever thought you would this side of Bassmasters.

3. **Treasure hunt.** Ask your toddler to find and bring back leaves, pebbles, acorns, and so on. Be careful of animal poop and garbage. Bring wipes!

4. **Follow the leader.** Everyone takes turns being the leader through the yard. This works better if there isn't just you and one kid, or it'll get old faster than last night's broccoli.

5. **Run.** Like horses, toddlers need a good run now and then.

Boys Will Be Boys and
Girls Will Be Girls

WHEN MY BOYS were little, we spent a lot of time sitting on the edge of our property, throwing rocks down the drainage ditch. My neighbor, Grace, pulled up one day with a minivan full of girls.

"What are you doing?" she asked, as though we were up to something absolutely ridiculous. When I explained that we were throwing rocks down the ditch, she just shook her head and drove off. It wasn't until she had a son a few years later that she understood why we spent so much time looking down drainpipes.

It's true that some boys play with dolls and some girls love trucks. But even kids as young as toddlers will play mostly along gender lines. I tried giving my boys a doll to play with, but they were far more interested in sticking it in the bed of their toy dump truck and delivering it along with some blocks and a few drink coasters from the coffee table. My niece, on the other hand, pushed her doll in a toy baby stroller wherever she went. And how thrilled was I to help carry it down a mall escalator shortly after my boys had given up their double stroller? Not very.

If your son takes a liking to traditionally girlie toys, don't fret. Likewise, don't panic if your daughter hates dolls. I never liked dolls, and I later managed to raise two babies nevertheless. Just let your toddlers play.

> **It worked for me!**
>
> "I have taken a roll of brown packing paper and covered my coffee table with it. It is exactly the right width and he can just color away without worrying about getting it on the table."
>
> —*Michelle, Sarasota, Florida*

"Shhh! Don't tell anyone, but Diego twenty-minute videos are my best-kept secret."

—*Sachia, Independence, Missouri*

It worked for me!

Hello? Toddlers Love to Play Telephone

AT FIRST, IT was adorable when your toddler pretended to use your cell phone. If nothing else, it provided a respite from entertaining him while you were trying to find some pj's in size 2T. Think of how many aisles you could get through at Target without a fuss thanks to your cell phone. What a relief!

But then your toddler's fun little hobby turns into an obsession, and before you know it, your cell phone or BlackBerry becomes one expensive, breakable toy with wet graham cracker crumbs crammed into its buttons and little fingerprints all over its screen. Pretty soon your toddler is walking around his playgroup, shouting into your phone like Tom Cruise in *Jerry Maguire*. And if you try to take it away, he throws a fit, jumping on the furniture like Tom Cruise on *Oprah*. What can you do? You can just say "no."

You can't let your toddler play with your phone just so you can get through the supermarket in peace and then expect him to understand why he can't play with it elsewhere. Your phone is off-limits to your toddler *all of the time*, no matter how desperate you are at Stop & Shop. Rather, give him a toy cell phone.

Toddlers love to imitate grown-up behaviors, so let him pick another one, such as pretending to cook with your pots and pans or "helping" you dust or sweep. It lets him get it out of his system while protecting your pricey gadgets.

And Now a Word from Our Sponsors

HERE'S THE DIRTY little secret nobody wants you to know: most moms use TV to entertain their toddlers now and then, even though the American Academy of Pediatrics says that kids under two shouldn't watch TV at all, and even though TV has practically become a bad word in some parenting circles.

But here's what the AAP doesn't recognize: sometimes you just need to cook dinner in peace or put your feet up longer than it takes to read a board book and—gasp!—do something that doesn't enrich your toddler's every waking moment.

Certainly, if your kids—of any age—watch so much TV they've memorized all the commercials for Bob's Furniture, they're watching too much. And if your toddler has seen more arrests on *Cops* than actual cops have experienced, perhaps there's a more appropriate show for her to watch.

But plopping your toddler down in front of the TV when you're under the weather or tired of being a guest at a stuffed animal tea party once again, or when your toddler is just plain cranky, is perfectly acceptable.

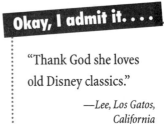

Okay, I admit it. . . .

"Thank God she loves old Disney classics."

—*Lee, Los Gatos, California*

Used with discretion, the TV is, in my opinion, a perfectly fine entertainer for your toddler—also, for you.

WE ASKED: What's the worst piece of advice anybody ever gave you about bringing up a toddler?

"Don't allow them to have many toys. Please . . . in today's society? Ya, right!"

—*Jennifer, Flemington, New Jersey*

Play Away

HOWEVER YOU DECIDE to entertain your toddler, remember that the toddler years are all about play . . . and potty training and socialization, too, but play is how they learn. If you set up your toddler with some fun toys and some time-killing activities, you'll both have a better time in the toddler years.

Gimme a break

Let Them Play

You don't have to micromanage your toddler's play all the time. If you let her play by herself now and then, she'll learn to entertain herself, thereby giving you a break whenever she digs into the toy box.

Just a Minute!

Animal Kingdom Profile: The Toddler

Known to make loud noises in quiet places, the resourceful toddler is among the few humans that can amuse him- or herself for an hour with nothing more than some Tupperware and your slippers.

Toddlers can be quick runners, especially if they spot a display case filled with sprinkle-covered cookies clear across the mall. On average, they sleep eleven hours a night and up to three hours a day, except, of course, when you really need some time to get your taxes done.

Toddlers don't always respond to logic, unless you consider insisting on riding in the stroller with your feather duster logical. Unlike their older counterparts, however, they will greet you like you're Elvis whenever you walk in the room.

Scientific Name

Toddleridis Tantrumlikelyus

Diet

Chicken nuggets, macaroni and cheese (shaped like Sponge-Bob), hot dogs, juice, Cheerios, grilled cheese (no crusts), and cookies.

Predators

The dog, who likes to chew on pacifiers and those cute little light-up Disney Princess sandals you just bought on sale, is really more of a nuisance than a predator. But other toddlers, who think "parallel play" means, "I play with everything while you stand parallel to me, not touching anything," can be dangerous.

Habitat

The playground, the backseat of your minivan, the couch in the family room, inside the toy box, and—in the wee hours of the night when you're too tired to object—your bed.

Range

From the upstairs bathroom all the way outside to the middle of your flowerbeds, if you're not fast enough to grab him in time.

Special Adaptations

Toddlers can learn very quickly. They will, for instance, repeat words you say when you've dropped a jar of pasta sauce on your foot—clearly and loudly—even when the rest of their vocabulary consists simply of "Dada" and "wheel."

They can climb over the crib rail and open the front door in the time it takes you to figure out that the person ringing the doorbell isn't the pizza guy after all. Reports of toddlers scaling kitchen counters to pilfer the Halloween candy you thought you had hidden so well behind the coffee maker is not uncommon.

Warnings

Approach with caution if you happen upon a toddler at nap time, balloon tied to one hand, and cake icing smeared across her face, having a major meltdown at a McDonald's PlayPlace. Also, toddlers are quite capable of making you forget they ripped up the mortgage bill by hugging you and cooing, "I wuv you, Mommy."

Chapter Ten

All in the Family
Your Toddler's Siblings, Grandparents, and Other Family Members

> **It worked for me!**
>
> "My son used to use [the baby's] nursing time to try and get away with things like jumping off the couch. I got up, with my daughter still nursing, and got him. I think he was amazed that Mommy got up because he didn't think I would."
>
> —Julie, West Chester, Pennsylvania

I could tell by the look on my toddler's face that he wasn't sure what all the fuss was about. His dad and grandparents were all huddled around me in my hospital bed while I held what must have appeared to him to be a red, wailing

165

bundle of noise. Just as someone snapped a photo, he looked up from his new little brother with an expression that said, "We aren't keeping that thing, are we?" Even now, there are days he'd like to send him back.

Until his brother was born, my nineteen-month-old was the center of his universe. The first grandchild on my husband's side, Nicholas was occasionally treated like the second coming of the Messiah, or close to it. I'm surprised trumpets didn't announce his arrival at family gatherings.

So when his little brother arrived, it rocked his world. He went from the center of the universe to something more akin to Pluto. Luckily, he was too young to get too jealous. Frankly, I don't think he was sure what was going on—until his little brother got big enough to touch his toys, that is. That's when the novelty of the red, wailing bundle of noise wore off, and the sibling rivalry wore on.

Whether you've added a baby to your family or your toddler has older siblings, he's got to learn to deal with them. And you've got to deal, not only with sibling rivalry, but Grandma's spoiling, Uncle Mike's "pull my finger" jokes, and a whole lot more. Your toddler and your family: perfect together? We'll see.

It worked for me!

"My parents always try to back us as parents, and so do my hubby's. They'll say, 'Your mommy said you can't do that.'"

—*Dawn, Lakewood, Ohio*

WE ASKED: How have your other family members hindered your parenting of a toddler?

"Two words: junk food!"

—*Susan, Edwardsville, Illinois*

Your Toddler, Your Family, Your Sanity . . . or Lack Thereof

MY MOTHER-IN-LAW was like the cavalry: she was going to swoop in and save me from calamity. But first, I'd have to spend an hour alone with my newborn and my toddler for the very first time. Shortly after my husband left for work that morning, all hell broke loose.

Rather than drag a newborn and a toddler all the way upstairs for a diaper change, I decided to lay my newborn down on the floor and change him there. Meanwhile, my nineteen-month-old decided to spin around in circles nearby. We all had our thing to do.

Everything was going great until Big Brother got dizzy and accidentally bumped into Little Brother, who started crying—and peeing straight up into the air. Realizing what he'd done, my toddler started crying, too, and soon I was sobbing along with both of them. When my mother-in-law showed up soon thereafter, I'd felt as though John Wayne had ridden in on horseback to pitch in on the homestead. My hero!

But when I had toddlers under my roof, it wasn't always one big happy family. And chances are it's the same way for you. What can you do?

WE ASKED: What kinds of issues did you deal with between your toddler and older siblings?

Jealousy: 41.7%

Always dragging my toddler to my older kids' activities: 58%

I can't help out at school because I have a toddler: 58%

I couldn't keep a nap schedule because of my older kids' schedules: 50%

My older kids hate when my toddler touches their stuff: 50%

My older kids hate when my toddler tries to play with them and their friends: 25%

It's hard to childproof; my older kids forget to shut doors, etc.: 33%

WE ASKED: What's the most difficult part of managing your toddler's relationship with older siblings?

"Explaining to the two-year-old that he just can't do the same things a four-year-old can."

—Chrissy, Dillsburg, Pennsylvania

Big Sis, Big Bro

MY YOUNGER SON didn't get much of his own mommy time until his big brother went off to preschool. By then, he'd learned to share me with an older sibling who didn't want him to touch the truck he was playing with or sit in my lap at the pediatrician's office. (I learned to balance two toddlers on one leg while filling out paperwork at the same time. Can I put that on a resume?) But older siblings present unique issues for your toddler. Here's how to deal with them.

He's Touching My Things!

No matter how much older your toddler's siblings are, chances are they don't want their runny-nosed, grubby-handed little sister to touch their stuff. Minimize it by:

- Keeping dangerous and breakable items out of your toddler's reach, such as older siblings' pencil sharpeners and handheld video games.

- Putting toys that belong to older siblings in separate toy boxes, closets, high shelves, or other containers.

- Keeping your toddler out of his siblings' rooms, even if it means letting them close the door on him.

- Not forcing your older kids to share certain things with your toddler. (If they're being just plain ridiculous by insisting they want to play with the Elmo/blocks/coaster/tissue box/whatever your toddler was headed toward, and you know they're just doing it to rile her up, that's a different story.)

- Letting the kid who touched it first play with it first for a set amount of time before turning it over. Using a timer will help train your toddler not to stand next to the child with the coveted item, stamping his feet and screeching.

She Won't Leave Us Alone!

Your toddler thinks that her sister and her sister's playdate are there to play with her, but the big kids would much rather go jump on the trampoline without worrying they're going to send a toddler into orbit. Fix it by:

- Giving your toddler some one-on-one mommy time while the big kids play. Create some special activities just for you and your toddler, including baking together, reading his favorite books, or playing dress-up.

- Inviting another toddler over to keep your tot's attention on his own toys and friends.

- Letting the big kids play behind closed doors, assuming they're old enough not to require eagle-eye supervision.

- Taking your toddler outdoors when the big kids are indoors and vice versa, depending on age appropriateness and neighborhood safety.

Do You Have to Bring Him Along?

Older siblings probably don't want a toddler running through their soccer practice or hanging out with their buddies on the beach. Make it easier by:

- Leaving your toddler at home with Daddy, Grandma, or a sitter.

- Keeping your toddler entertained (and therefore out of her sibling's stuff and business) with her own toys and activities. Yes, even if this means you spend the first three innings of your son's baseball game chasing a tot-size soccer ball near the snack stand.

- Sharing the carpooling with other moms for the older kids' activities, so you can stay home with just your toddler now and then.

She Started It!

You're going to hear this one for a long, long time. You turn around just as one kid clocks the other, so you punish him, and then he shouts it isn't fair because your toddler started it. Nip it in the bud by:

- Having a zero tolerance for pushing, hitting, and so on, even if it's the little one smacking the big one. Sternly, but calmly, warn the offender not to hit and remove her from the room for a short time-out.

- Not refereeing. Unless things are getting so heated that hitting might soon follow, stay out of your kids' conflicts and see if they can work things out for themselves. If you need to step in, there's no point in getting to the bottom of who did what (unless someone has clearly injured someone else). Just break it up and move on. If you always jump in to referee, you'll find yourself the star of your very own *Judge Judy* show.

- Splitting them up. Remember what your mom told you: "If you can't play nicely, you can't play at all."

Help! I Can't Keep a Nap Schedule

Your older kids' schedules are making it tough for your toddler to nap. What can you do? Trade carpooling with another mom who has a toddler. One drives, the other watches over the nappers. Or ask Grandma or Grandpa or hire a reliable sitter to stay with your toddler during nap time.

Okay, I admit it. . . .

"My younger child really looked up to her older brother and always wanted to do whatever he was doing. He didn't think this was as cute as I did."

—*Angie,*
Hayden Lake, Idaho

WE ASKED: What issues did you have to deal with when you gave your toddler a younger sibling?

I felt guilty for not being able to give my toddler attention: 69%

Changing two (or more) sets of diapers each day: 54%

Jealousy: 31%

Worrying my toddler would get the baby sick: 23%

The baby woke up my toddler at night: 15%

My toddler wouldn't potty train or had setbacks: 15%

I couldn't take my toddler anywhere because of the baby: 15%

"Alexander came to the hospital with Daddy to bring Mommy and the new baby home. We called the baby his baby so he felt ownership of him."

It worked for me!

—*Lynn, Belton, Missouri*

And Baby Makes Four (or Five, Six. . . .)

HERE'S HOW YOU know you're supertired: you change the baby's diaper twice in a matter of minutes and leave your toddler altogether diaperless. I discovered this very mistake when I realized that my toddler was wandering around the family room with his snaps undone and fresh pee staining his jumpsuit. I'd forgotten to finish changing his diaper, instead changing his little brother's diaper twice for no apparent reason other than I was deliriously tired and temporarily confused. Good thing my nineteen-month-old was too young to get jealous. Besides, I think he liked the nice breeze he was getting up his unsnapped pants.

A friend who is the mother of triplets once told me, "I'd rather have triplets than a toddler and a baby." I felt both vindicated and hopeless at the same time. A seasoned mother of triplets said she'd rather have three babies than a toddler and a newborn under her roof. Huh?

But now that I've made it through those years, I can see what she was saying. Adding a baby when you're deep into the toddler years is a bit insane, or at least it feels that way when you're changing the wrong diapers. But it also has its advantages, like when your kids share clothes, toys, friends, and even sports teams when they get older. Here are some tips for caring for your toddler after little brother or sister is born.

When Your Toddler Is Jealous

One day, your toddler is the center of attention and the reason for everything that happens in the house. The next, there's a new baby in the house, and everyone is oohing and aahing and generally ignoring your poor toddler, who probably feels like she's been knocked off *American Idol* by some up-and-coming, no-good, talentless singer who seemed to come out of nowhere. Curb her jealousy by:

• Preparing her for the new baby ahead of time. Spend time with other people's babies, read her books on being the big sister, and talk (very excitedly) about how your toddler will be the big kid in the family. Even young toddlers understand "baby." And if you can sell them on the idea that a new baby means great stuff for them, the transition will go as smoothly as possible.

• Showering him with gifts. Make sure he gets some big brother goodies from relatives and from you when you bring the baby home. It'll not only make him feel special, it'll keep his mind off all the new baby fuss. Who doesn't like new toys?

• Never blaming any disappointments on the baby. If you tell your toddler she can't go to the playground because the baby needs his nap, you're only fueling the jealousy fire. Just tell her you'll go to the playground later and divert her attention with something else equally fun. Toddlers have a short attention span. Use it to your advantage.

• Spending alone time with him. Ease his fear of displacement by reassuring him that he's still loved. My husband spent extra time with our older son while I tended to the newborn. But I also made sure my toddler and I had time alone together whenever I could, especially during the baby's morning nap. He also got a lot of alone time with his grandmothers, who, frankly, spoiled him during the time they were together, thereby making *me* a little jealous.

Smack! Waaaaaa! When Toddlers Lash Out

Your kids are going to wallop each other over the years, but your baby is no match for a walking, whacking toddler. Prevent trouble by:

- Never leaving your toddler alone with the baby. Even if she doesn't have an evil plot to harm the baby, her well-meaning help (such as "feeding" the baby her snacks) just might.

- Never telling your toddler he's in charge of the baby. He's too little to baby-sit, and he should never think he can take over for you. Thank him for handing you the soap, but don't ever say, "Ryan is in charge of the baby's bath." He might believe it.

- Never laughing when your toddler hits you. Teach him he can't hit anyone, so he doesn't try to hit the baby.

When Your Toddler Won't Potty Train Anymore

Now that the baby is here, your otherwise potty-trained toddler has suddenly boycotted the toilet in favor of crouching behind the couch and pooping in her pants. Deal with potty-training setbacks by:

- Never punishing her for regressing. Like you, she is dealing with a huge life change. Potty-training setbacks are normal and fixable. Never let her see you're upset about them. Just clean up the messes matter-of-factly. If things really get bad, fall back on training pants for a while and then start up the potty training again later.

• Pointing out that the baby is too little to use the toilet, but that your toddler doesn't have to stay "all yucky" in a poopy or wet diaper. It'll appeal to her sense of "I'm the big sister" pride. But be careful: some toddlers regress because they see all the fuss the baby is getting. If she seems to hate the idea of being the big sister, don't use this tactic, as it'll only make things worse.

• Letting him take a break from potty training. If your toddler was potty training when the baby was born, you might consider letting him have a vacation from potty training until this stressful time is over. Don't make a big deal out of it. Just start back up again when he's more used to having little sister around.

> **It worked for me!**
>
> "My mother-in-law would watch the little one one day a week for me, so I could go and volunteer in the older ones' classrooms."
>
> —Angie, Hayden Lake, Idaho

Momma Said

WE ASKED: How have your other family members hindered your parenting of a toddler?

"They blamed me for having a screaming brat. Of course, I had twins, and so at least I had my daughter for Exhibit B as proof that I wasn't ruining [my son]."

—Sharon, Port Orange, Florida

Gwandma! And Other Family Members
Who Help or Hinder

EVERY WEEK, MY mother-in-law spent a few hours with my toddlers, so I could go wander around the mall and talk to myself. When I returned, my kids would be well behaved and content, which, of course, made me both happy and ticked off at the same time.

How did she do that? How did my mother-in-law tame the Terrible Twos, make potty training seem a breeze, and get my picky eater to ingest things he deemed "yucky, no!" whenever I served them to him? It was fascinating as well as maddening, but I never told her that. Instead, I thanked her and set my sights on the next time I could buy myself a latte and walk around aimlessly, thanks to my mother-in-law.

Whether your relatives make things easier or harder while you try to parent a toddler probably varies day to day. One day your brother does a fabulous job of filling in for you while you go get your bangs cut, so you no longer look like a sheepdog, and the next, he has the bright idea to teach your toddler to quote Bart Simpson: "I will not draw naked ladies in class." Whether your family members work with you or against you when it comes to parenting your toddler, you've got to figure out how to make sure your toddler's best interests are at hand. Here are the top five issues you might face:

1. **Whoa! Your toddler's safety is at risk.** Your parents might remind you that they raised you, and you turned out perfectly fine, but those were different times, back when kids

ambled about untethered in the car and nobody thought twice about letting a toddler hang out in the backyard "supervised" by the big kids—a kindergartener and two third-graders with hockey sticks. What can you do?

Make safety rules and stick to them. Anyone else who cares for your toddler must adhere to your safety rules, even if they think that safety gates are silly. If your parents or anyone else watching your toddler can't follow your safety rules, don't leave your toddler alone with them.

2. **Our way or the highway:** They tell you how to parent—and you don't like it. A little tried-and-true advice is fine with you, but your in-laws like to tell you how you're parenting your toddler all wrong. They make you feel like every bad behavior your toddler exhibits is all your fault. Is your toddler biting? It's because you let him watch too much TV. Not potty training yet? Maybe if you gave up your job and stayed home with him. Screeching like a howler monkey over the toy they just took away from him? Yep, your fault, too. How do you handle this one?

Shout it out loud or suck it up. Yes, I just gave conflicting advice, but here's why: some things aren't worth fighting about. If your in-laws are undermining your authority by letting your toddler have the lollipop you just refused her, by all means, speak up. You are the parent here, and your rules go, so that your toddler learns to respect you. But if your in-laws insist your toddler should wear a jacket even though you think it's a bit warm outside, shut up and put the jacket on him. They'll appreciate the moral victory, and you and your toddler lose nothing in the process.

3. **Clueless: They don't know how to handle a toddler.**
Your sister has a baby who, so far, is as animated as a throw pillow. Though she's a mother, Sis has no idea how to handle a toddler who is trying to hop on top of the dog like the Lone Ranger on Silver. Away! You don't want to hurt your sister's feelings or her pride, but sheesh, would it hurt her to get out of her chair and follow your toddler to the eye-level window openers before the kid pokes her eye out? What can you do?

Treat them like decorative powder room soaps—nice, but not really all that useful. Unless you leave your sister alone with your toddler for a few days with nothing but a diaper bag and a pantry full of mac 'n' cheese, she's just not going to get it. Certainly, when it comes to safety, make some suggestions to her, such as, "Um, Sis? Could you shut the door to the basement before Hannah tumbles down the stairs?" But otherwise treat her as though she is there only for conversation and to pass the mashed potatoes. When her baby becomes a toddler, she'll learn—and won't that feel good?

4. **That's not how we do it! Their parenting philosophies differ from yours.** You think it's okay to put nap time off for thirty minutes while your toddler and his cousin play

nicely, but your brother-in-law is mortified. Nap time is at
1:00 PM sharp in his house, no matter what's going on in the
rest of the world. He scoops up his toddler and puts him
down for a nap while your toddler makes that face that precedes a knock-down, drag-out, "I'm really tired and mad"
temper tantrum. How do you handle it?

Their kid. Their rules. You might think it's ridiculous
that your nephew can't have any cookies at any time no
matter if all the rest of the kids at the birthday party are so
happily chomping on their Chips Ahoys. But don't mess
with their rules. You have your rules, after all, and you
expect other family members to respect them. As long as
their rules don't interfere with your own when it comes to
your toddler, let it go. Also, adjust accordingly so that at the
next family gathering, your toddler isn't left to wonder why
his cousin was relocated just when things were getting fun.

5. **Uninvited. When your toddler isn't included in the family
   fun.** All the big kids are going outside to use your niece's
   new skateboarding ramp, but your toddler isn't invited—
   again. They leave her out of everything from playing in the
   yard to watching movies in the family room. You thought
   the family get-together would have more getting together
   for your toddler, but you're realizing now that she's too
   young to partake in a lot of the fun—and it's breaking her
   heart. What can you do?

Be a toddler tour guide. Certainly you can understand why the big kids don't want a toddler hanging around. And frankly, you should be relieved they didn't try to send your toddler headfirst down the ramp on a skateboard. But you can come up with some activities that everyone can do, such as piling in the cars to go get ice cream together or even cooking together. (Give your toddler her own bowl to mess around in while the bigger kids do the real work.) Then let the big kids be big kids and play one-on-one with your toddler. Better yet, let her have Grandma to herself for a while.

> "Once a month or so, he [Daddy] picks up our four-year-old daughter from school and takes her out for lunch. He started when she was three and will start with our son next year."
>
> —Chrissy, Dillsburg, Pennsylvania

It worked for me!

What About Daddy?

WHILE MUCH MORE is expected of fathers today, let's face it: some dads are lost when it comes to caring for the kids, especially a toddler. And if you've hogged the baby until now, he probably hasn't learned much, either. You can help Daddy care for your toddler by:

- Letting him make mistakes. You might be a superior diaperer, and you sure can fold the stroller with one hand while holding a toddler with the other, but let Daddy figure it all out on his own. Unless your toddler's safety is at risk, let him parent his own way.

- Not rescuing him. Don't swoop in to help your hubby unless he asks for it. He needs to endure a few temper tantrums and runny noses to prepare him for many more years of parenting ahead.

- Not badmouthing him. If you tell everyone Hubby is a useless clod, he'll start to believe it, and so will everyone else. Then you'll be left to wonder why you have to do the dirty work all the time. Because Hubby's a useless clod, remember? You started it.

- Giving him his own star billing. Let Daddy be in charge of bath time or a Saturday morning trip to the bagel shop with your toddler. It'll give them both some time together.

- Never using the word "help." When you say Daddy's "helping," you imply that he's doing you a favor. Give him partnership in parenting by giving him his own responsibilities.

- Having a united front. If your discipline styles don't match, don't let your toddler know it. You need to work out a plan for doling out the discipline and then stick to it, even if it means finding a happy medium between your styles.

- Finding time for the two of you. Set up a regular date night where you can get out, just the two of you. And try not to talk about the kids the whole time.

- Penciling in sex. If you wait for it to happen, it probably won't. But if you plan ahead, you'll find the time (and the energy) for each other.

"I depend on my husband a lot, and I think that benefits our whole family. Taking care of the children strengthened the bond between them."

—Anne, West Milford, New Jersey

It worked for me!

Gimme a break

Make Time for Hubby

For years, my husband and I had a movie night—at home. Every Friday night, we'd rent a grown-up movie, send the kids to bed, and enjoy our time together. We didn't have to get a sitter, and it cost only the price of the movie rental. And it was a nice break for both of us. Start your movie night, too. You never know what it'll lead to.

Just a minute!

YOU'RE INVITED

What: A sentence-finishing party

Where: The living room

When: After the kids (finally) go to sleep

Join me as we attempt to hold a
conversation that isn't interrupted by refilling sippy cups,
preventing small objects from going up nostrils,
and mad dashes to the potty.

*R.S.V.P. by 8:30 PM, or before I start getting
that look in my eyes that precedes deep, drooling sleep.*

B.Y.O.V. (Bring Your Own Verbs)

Chapter Eleven

Pick, Pick, Pick
The Milestones You Don't Want to Share with Grandma

 WE ASKED: What's the worst part of having a toddler?

"Maintaining control throughout a tantrum when all you want to do is scream at/with them."

—*Stacy, Fort Wayne, Indiana*

My son's milestones book had no special sticker for "Climbs out of Crib." It had stickers for the usual milestones, such as: "Rolls Over," "First Word," and "Walks." But none for "Scales Down His Crib Rails Like Spiderman on the Chrysler Building."

Had I not been so very pregnant at the time of his first great escape, I might have reached him before his twenty-six-pound body made a loud THUD on his bedroom floor. Instead, I watched helplessly as my fifteen-month-old walked off the video baby monitor screen and over to work on his next milestone that has no sticker, "Opens Doors."

Worse, my mother-in-law was there to witness it. One minute, Omi's sweet little "gold fogel" (golden bird) was sound asleep, and the next, he was staging a great escape. And I couldn't do anything about it except beat him to the stairs. Barely.

After that episode, I got smart and installed a gate at the top of the stairway. And yet that didn't stop my next toddler, whose milestone book should have included this unique sticker: "Squeezes Through Stair Rails to Retrieve a Power Bar from the Kitchen Table While Mommy Showers, Oblivious." I know, because he handed me the snack he apparently had hankered for while I was toweling off. And boy was he proud. If I had a Mommy Milestone book, I would have used up my own unique sticker: "Discovers that Child-proofing Works Only on the Cat."

"Keeps Mommy on Her Toes"

MY SISTER-IN-LAW had no idea how good she had had it with her daughter until her son came along. "Emily never dipped her hands in the dog bowl," she told me when her son was a newly mobile toddler. "And she never climbed up high on the furniture, either." I couldn't help but laugh nervously, because my sons had long out-grown those years, and yet I remember them well, like my final exam in microeconomics—long over, but still sharply painful.

We certainly aren't the only parents to get blindsided by toddler antics. When my cousin had a toddler living under his roof, he told me, "I turned around for just a second and when I turned back, he was standing smack in the middle of the kitchen table." I chuckled, remembering how we removed the coffee table from the family room in the vacation house we visited one summer, just in case my toddlers got the same idea. Fool me once, shame on you. Fool me twice, and clearly I've got a toddler in the house.

But it's not so funny when you're going through it, is it? I remember watching the McCaughey septuplets swarming around the stage on *Oprah* just after their first birthday and thinking, *Can toddlers trigger vertigo?* Because if I had to keep an eye on seven toddlers at once, I'd certainly feel dizzy. How many beads could they shove up their noses in one day? I shuddered at the thought. That day, I created my own mantra designed to help me get through the toddler years: "At least there aren't seven of him."

Yet all it takes is just one toddler to keep you on your toes. What can you expect when you least expect it?

Milestone: Opens, Closes, Locks, and Unlocks Doors

ONE MORNING, I went upstairs to put my son Christopher, then ten months old, down for a nap, when I glanced out the window to see someone running up the front walkway. "Gee," I mumbled. "That guy's in a hurry." Well, "that guy" turned out to be my two-year-old son, Nicholas, who had apparently mastered opening doors while I was heading up the stairs. Next milestone: ringing doorbells.

Lucky for me, nobody else had witnessed his one-hundred-yard dash, though for months afterward, I feared the UPS guy would deliver my toddler to my front door along with my packages and a stern look of disapproval.

Even better, I didn't have to endure the embarrassment—and fear—one of my friends experienced when her toddler locked her out of the house. When she couldn't coax her daughter to "open the door for Mommy now!" she had to rush over to the neighbor's house and call 911. The police and the fire department came out to open her door for her and her groceries, while neighbors watched, no doubt shaking their heads and wondering how that woman let a two-year-old lock her out of her own house. After that, she never left the house again without her keys in her pocket and a sense of acute readiness not uncommon among Marines in combat.

Why do toddlers love to open and close, lock and unlock doors, especially when you don't want them to? Because they can and because it bothers you. It's their way of testing their boundaries, along with your patience. The key is to make sure they can't ever move that boundary without your consent. And take heart: at least there aren't seven of them.

What Can You Do?

- Childproof your doors using plastic doorknob covers or bolts high above your toddler's reach.

- Add door alarms, especially for doors that lead outside or to the garage.

- Hang a towel over room-to-room doors inside the house to keep your toddler's fingers from being trapped.

- Keep a key to the house and your cell phone in your pocket or a key hidden outside in case your toddler decides to try the lock when you step outside for a minute.

WE ASKED: What kinds of things does your toddler do that drive you up a wall?

Doesn't listen to "no!": 63%

Runs away, especially in public places: 58%

Insist on doing things themselves, even if it takes forever: 53%

Temper tantrums: 47%

Squirms during diaper changes or fights getting into car seat: 37%

Figures out how to get around childproofing: 26%

Picks nose: 26%

Plays with the toilet: 21%

Imitates your bad behaviors (cursing, burping, etc.): 21%

Says "no!" all too often: 21%

Climbs up on furniture, etc.: 21%

Opens and closes doors/locks: 16%

Fascinated with body parts (his/hers or others): 16%

Stuffs things up nose, in ears, etc.: 5%

Takes off clothes: 5%

Milestone: Discovers Body Parts—
Theirs or Someone Else's

DO YOU HAVE one of those toddlers who seems fixated on body parts—and I don't mean earlobes? The boy who takes every opportunity to make sure his johnson is still in full swing, or the girl who asks the mailman if he has a vajajay, too? Or maybe your toddler is more interested in his playdate's parts than in his own. Look on the bright side: they're not teenagers yet.

To you, it might feel like an unhealthy public obsession with some very private parts. But to your toddler, it's all about finding out how their bodies work.

What Can You Do?

If you gasp and chastise your toddler to "never, ever flash your pee-pee at the school bus again," you're just encouraging more of his behavior. To your toddler, there's nothing more fun than exploring his body except exploring his body *and* seeing Mommy nearly have a nervous breakdown because of it.

Instead of reacting like your toddler has just learned to juggle with steak knives and a chainsaw, divert his attention with another activity. Or just shout,

Okay, I admit it. . . .

"My son is discovering how boy's bodies can 'change.' He gets very mad and pulls his pants down and announces to anyone in earshot what's going on. It's funny but something that can't continue!"

—*Angie,*
Indianapolis, Indiana

"Look! Is that a puppy over there?" Whatever you decide to do, make sure you're distracting your toddler without making his one-man exploration seem like something truly naughty and, therefore, attractive.

Keep in mind that you should never make your child's behavior seem shameful. Instead, teach your children about *all* their body parts, so they don't get overly interested in the private ones—or someone else's private ones.

WE ASKED: What's the worst part about having a toddler?

"The frustration of wanting to help but knowing they needed to do things on their own."

—*Amy, League City, Texas*

Milestone: The "I Do It!" Syndrome

IT'S TIME TO leave, but your toddler has insisted on zippering her jacket, even though she really has no clue how to do it all that well. You're starting to sweat in your winter coat and wool hat. You glance at the clock and then look back at your toddler, who's still struggling with the zipper. You shift the baby on your hip and ask in the most pleasant *Mommy-loves-you!* voice you can summon, "Would you like Mommy to help you with that?"

Suddenly your sweet little one in the pink and purple Dora the Explorer boots has turned into Linda Blair in *The Exorcist.* She looks up from her zipper with evil in her eyes and shouts, "I do it!" If you wait long enough, her head just might spin around and bats will fly through the window. And that would certainly make you late.

Nobody knows how many hours or how much patience has been lost to the "I Do It!" syndrome throughout the history of motherhood, but we've all wondered why our toddlers insist on doing things they can't when anyone else would ask for help. (Well, anyone except men who are lost while driving, but that's why they invented GPS.)

To you, it's another exhausting thing that's keeping you from getting to Mommy and Me class on time yet again. But to your toddler, it's all about asserting some independence by taking on greater tasks, such as dressing herself or doing her own hair. Remember that she just doesn't understand that some tasks could prove dangerous in her hands. (Think of those local news stories: "Toddler gets stuck on airport luggage conveyor belt! Film at eleven.") Nor does she understand that you feel like you're going to melt into the doorway while you wait for her to figure out the @#$! zipper.

What Can You Do?

Give her a little controlled independence. Set aside a day each week that your child can plan her own wardrobe—even if that means taking her to the playground in her Cinderella Halloween costume. Allot extra time whenever you have to go somewhere, in case she wants to spend five minutes trying to fasten her car seat belts herself. Meanwhile, if your cell phone has Solitaire on it, enjoy!

You'll need to be extra diligent about childproofing by locking up tubes, jars, and bottles out of reach, because your toddler might start getting into what she never seemed to be interested in before. Also, keep the phone number for Poison Control handy. And breathe deeply and evenly. You'll need the patience.

> **It worked for me!**
>
> "I am most surprised with how much toddlers can do if given the chance. My son can feed himself with a fork and spoon, and do a decent job with it. I gave him more opportunities to try these things, let him feed himself less messy things, and he did great!"
>
> —Kellie, Derby, Connecticut

Milestone: Toilet Games

MY TODDLERS BOTH went through a phase where, to them, the toilet wasn't a waste receptacle, but rather a place to dip toy trucks. I thought it might be a sign that they're ready to potty train, but they thought of it as a wonderful place to splash around at a moment's notice—sometimes, for instance, when I didn't notice.

Many toddlers love water, especially the swirling kind, and the toilet is the perfect height for a toddler to use as a toy. When you're two, oh, how much fun it is to watch the water disappear down the drain! Also, the decorative soaps! And Baby Gap socks! And a couple of pacifiers and a rubber ball! But what a mess for you.

Minimally, you're looking at bathroom floor and toddler clean-up. Worst-case scenario, you're calling the plumber.

What Can You Do?

You can get it out of their system by allowing them to play in water elsewhere. I let my toddlers play with Tupperware in the kitchen sink. They filled and dumped various-size containers with water over and over until the toilet didn't seem as much fun to them. Yes, they got soaked—and so did my counters and the rug under their step stool—but it was far better than finding my boys' Thomas the Tank Engine toys in the toilet.

Of course, you should always supervise your children around water, no matter how shallow it is. And it wouldn't hurt to check the toilet for balls, blocks, toys, soap bars, a roll of toilet paper, kitty litter, car keys, mail, and who-knows-what-else before you flush, just in case.

Okay, I admit it. . . .

"I hated having to watch him every second to make sure he didn't hurt himself or throw my phone out in the diaper pail. I guess I didn't watch closely enough because we had to replace the phone."

—*Lisa, Blue Bell, Pennsylvania*

WE ASKED: What were the early signs that your toddler was asserting her/his independence?

"My daughter insisted on wearing Minnie Mouse ears everywhere she went for a week."

—*Anne, West Milford, New Jersey*

Milestone: Stuffing Things up
Noses and into Ears

I WAS RECUPERATING from minor same-day surgery in the hospital when I saw a mom and dad standing over their child, who was still asleep from surgery. The moment the boy woke up, his father held up a plastic container with a small black object in it, and barked, "Never, ever put this in your ear again!"

Turns out, the boy had broken a mirror off one of his toy cars, and instead of asking his parents to fix it, he stuffed it into his ear so far that it took surgery to remove it. I would ridicule his behavior, except my mother would most certainly bring up the Bead-up-the-Nose trick I had performed when I was that boy's age.

To toddlers, bodily orifices provide a handy, portable spot to stick things. Your toddler, who doesn't quite grasp actions-and-consequences yet, likely sees no difference in putting pegs in the holes of the toy you gave him for his birthday and shoving peas up his nostrils. Round things. Round holes. What fun!

What Can I Do?

You could get a frequent visitor card at the ER, or you can take some preemptive steps, including:

- Keep any alluring small items, such as beads, buttons, candy, pebbles, and pet food out of your toddler's reach unless under strict, eagle-eye adult supervision.

- Teach your kids that nothing smaller than their elbows should go into their noses or ears, no matter how much fun it might seem to shove Sparky's kibble up there.

If your toddler has already stuffed something in his ears or nose, take these steps:

1. Don't try to dig it out, because you might cause more trouble.

2. If it's in his nose, try to get him to blow it out, if he knows how.

3. Call your doctor or head to the emergency room.

WE ASKED: How did you maintain your sanity during some of the more trying days with your toddler?

"I felt better after having a good cry."

—*Mary, Chicago, Illinois*

WE ASKED: What one word or phrase would you use to describe the toddler stage?

"ARGH!"

—*Beth, Warrington, Pennsylvania*

Milestone: Picks Her Nose

SPEAKING OF PICKING, what do you do if your toddler discovers her fingers fit nicely up her nose, and chooses to try it out often? You can't take away her fingers, after all, or stuff them in boxing gloves all day.

Kids with allergies or colds are most likely to pick their nose because, well, there's stuff to pick up there. Some kids pick their noses simply because they can. It's something to do while she's waiting for her snack or—worse—for you to finish checking out at the supermarket.

What Can I Do?

Resist the urge to nag her about it. Chances are, she doesn't even realize she's doing it. Instead, quietly remove her fingers from her nose and say nothing at all. Then, keep her hands busy with a toy or a book. Most kids outgrow nose picking by the time they get to school, when, chances are, some kid will point at her and shout, "Gross! Ally picks her nose!"

But if she's drawing blood when she picks her nose, it might be a sign of a medical issue. If this happens, consult your pediatrician.

Milestone: Potty Language

THE GOOD THING about toddlers is that they don't know the lyrics to "The Diarrhea Song" yet, unless, of course, they've got ten-year-old brothers. But toddlers are like parrots in light-up sneakers. That's why your sweet little girl with the curls and tights and everything nice just might come home from dinner at Uncle Kevin's with a new word in her vocabulary: "crap." Worse, she wanders around your house, the mall, your playgroup, saying it over and over again, "Crap. Crap. Crap. Crap," while the other mommies snicker.

Oh, crap.

Chances are, your toddler has no idea what she's saying. She just likes the way it sounds and, more likely, the reaction she gets from grown-ups when she says it. At first, it's just another word to add to her vocabulary. But then it quickly becomes a great way to get Mommy to make that funny face while she's shouting.

What Can I Do?

Whatever you do, don't overreact. Don't yell, correct her, or even giggle, because let's face it, sometimes it's pretty darn funny to hear a kid whose entire vocabulary consists of about a dozen words shout "@#$%!" when she spills the Goldfish crackers.

> "If you don't want her to go around saying 'Oh, crap' in her little sing-song voice, it is best not to say it around her. I am constantly amazed at how much my toddler remembers about things now and picks up on what is going on around her."
>
> —*Leandra, Sumter, South Carolina*

It worked for me!

Instead, come up with an alternative word or words, such as "Uh-oh!" or "Oh no!" or "Whoopsies!" And while you're at it, change your vocabulary, too, so that the next time you drop a can of tomato sauce on your foot, you don't wind up teaching your toddler yet another colorful new word for her repertoire.

Milestone: Temper Tantrums

I SHOULD HAVE known better than to put the party hats back on the shelf where they belonged. My toddler had spread them out across the floor in the Party Favors aisle at Party City and, apparently, expected them to stay there, along with the plastic plates he'd carried over from another aisle and his Scooby-Doo book. So when I started to clean up the mess, he threw a fit. Well, not just a fit, but a knock-down, all-out temper tantrum, while I hid behind a Bon Voyage card and pretended not to know this very loud, very angry boy.

It's really not all that reassuring to hear, "All toddlers have tantrums," especially when you're enduring one in the middle of a public place while all the grandmas give you the look that says, "In our day, we knew how to control our children." But put yourself in your toddler's place: you can't speak very well, you're not all that coordinated, and somebody just ruined the masterpiece that you'd so painstakingly made. If you were two, you'd throw a tizzy, too.

What Can I Do?

You can't give him the Bon Voyage card, no matter how good that would make you feel. Besides, he can't read yet. (I, on the other hand, could have used a Cope card.) Instead, you can figure out what kind of tantrum he's having and help diffuse it.

Frustration fit. Your toddler is having a canary because he can't get the minibasketball into the cute little basket that came with it, no matter how many times he tries. Every time he misses the basket, he wails and kicks like a drunken fan at a Lakers game. When you try to help him make the shot, he gets even more frustrated, and soon, you've got one ticked-off toddler on your hands. What can you do?

Fix it and forget it. This is where the magical power of diversion comes in handy once again. You simply have to shift his attention to something more fun and less challenging than the stinkin' basketball toy, even if that means—gasp!—turning on the TV for half an hour or so.

Manipulative Meltdown. Your toddler really, really, *really* wants the giant lollipop shaped like Big Bird, and she wants it *now*. So she throws a hairy temper tantrum, complete with falling to the ground as though she's been shot and wounded, right there in the middle of Wal-Mart for all to see. She's hoping she'll persuade you (to use a popular euphemism for "extort") to give up and pay up for her lollipop. What do you do?

Just say "no"! Yes, she's going to kick and scream all the way to your car, but whatever you do, don't cave in, no matter how much you hate looking like a mean mom. If you let her have her way this time, you might as well program her public-place default setting to "Tantrum" for the rest of her toddler years.

"Most of the trying days come when you want them to do something, and they want to do something else. We turn things into a game, and the sanity returns, and everyone is happy and smiling as opposed to fussy and crying."

—*Karyn, Northville, Michigan*

It worked for me!

Gimme a break

Hide Online

The best part about the Internet is that it never closes. Anytime you're feeling overwhelmed by motherhood, you can find another mom just like you online, any time of the day. Join a few social networks or message boards geared toward moms of toddlers, and you'll find a nice safe place to "hide" from your toddler's antics any time of day.

Just a minute!

"I Do It!": A Real-World Milestone Sticker Book for Toddlers

Discovers that coins don't fit up nose, but beads from sister's jewelry-making kit do.

Locks door while Mommy stands in the garage, frantically searching for the spare key under the mat, which has gone missing.

- Discovers that key from under mat fits into the doorknob. Also, in the space between the heater and the wall.

- Flashes his winkie at neighbors passing by driveway while Mommy moves toward him faster than he's ever seen her go!

- Belches—just like Daddy, only, apparently, funnier.

- Melts into the bakery floor when Mommy refuses to let her have the jumbo iced Cookie Monster cookie.

- First Word: "Boobs."

- Second Word: "Fart," said repeatedly like Rain Man— "Fartfartfartfartfartfartfart."

- Answers the front door naked, like Paris Hilton on weekends.

- Picks nose.

- Picks dog's nose.

- Unlatches toilet lock faster than Houdini could escape from handcuffs.

- Brings Mommy picture that was hanging on the wall two feet over the new couch.

Chapter Twelve

Bwess You:
When Your Toddler Is Sick and
(Inevitably) When You Are, Too

My two-year-old was up early again. He was sick. I was sick. We were tired. So we lay on the couch together at 0-dark-thirty in the morning. I wiped his nose and blew my own while praying that he'd fall back asleep, so I could snooze until my other son awoke. Only fifteen hours until bedtime. Yippee!

Just as he seemed to doze off, I sneezed. I prepared to calm him back down when he lifted his head, looked me in the eye, and said, "Bwess you." Then he put his head back down while I blew my nose again.

Okay, I admit it. . . .

"I knew I was a mother when my toddler started to throw up on the couch and I put my hands out to catch it. *Ewww!*"

—*Chrissy,*
Dillsburg, Pennsylvania

Oh, the colds we've known—and the ear infections, croup, flu bugs, bronchitis, strep throat, stomach flu. Bwess me, indeed. And bwess my toddlers, too, for all their sneezes, coughs, throat cultures, and other rotten things for such little kids to have to endure.

What do you do when your toddler is sick? And what about when you're sick? You won't find medical advice here. I'll leave that up to the pediatricians and WebMD. Instead, I'll concentrate on how you deal with your toddler's illnesses—and your own. Bwess you.

Achoooo!

THE AVERAGE KID gets between six and ten colds a year, compared to adults, who normally get two to four. But "normally" no longer applies to you, because your toddler is sneezing on you and putting all sorts of household items in her mouth. Kids in day care and school usually get more colds—up to twelve per year. What's a momma to do?

Chances are you've already stocked up on some of the basics in your medicine cabinet for your baby. But now that you have a toddler who's on the go and into everything, she might catch things she didn't when she was a baby. And chances are, you will, too. Here are a few items to have on hand, just in case:

- **Vaporizer or humidifier.** Its moist air will help keep your toddler's nose and chest clear at night. I have found that humidifiers are hard to find in stores in the flu off-season, so to speak, so be on the lookout or search the Internet. There

are some fun-shaped humidifiers, including SpongeBob, a
penguin, and a soccer ball. Before you plunk down forty
bucks on a Thomas the Tank Engine vaporizer, keep in mind
that your kid might not love it anymore when he's ten.
Besides, if it looks like a toy, your toddler might want to play
with it. Check online reviews from customers to see how
well any humidifier really works in the trenches.

- **Saline spray.** As long as it's okay with your pediatrician, you
can help get some of those snoogies out of your toddler's
nose with a saline spray. It'll loosen up the mucus so you can
either suction it out with a bulb syringe, or, if you're lucky,
your toddler can blow it out.

- **Lots of tissues.** We're allergy sufferers here, so we always
have a lot of nice soft tissues on hand. If you don't blow your
nose as much as we do, please take my advice: don't buy the
cheap, rough tissues that seem like they came from behind
the Iron Curtain in 1963. Get the soft, cushy kind. We like
the ones with lotion in it, but then, we spoil ourselves with
our tissues because we sneeze so much.

- **Lots of rags at the ready.** Let's just say it's amazing how
much can come out of one small person who ate nothing
more than three peas and a chicken nugget for dinner.

- **A digital ear thermometer.** I don't know about you, but I
don't want to stick a thermometer you-know-where, especially if that "where" might be loaded. And my kids wouldn't

use the oral ones until they were in grade school. There's just something about sticking it under the tongue that can freak a kid out. Invest in a good digital ear thermometer. When your toddler is burning up with fever at 3:00 AM, you'll be happy you did.

- **Tummy meds.** I keep Emetrol on hand to help stop vomiting and nausea, assuming your toddler can get it down and keep it there. (Note: It's not made for kids under two.) Another option is Children's Maalox or Mylanta, which come in chewable tablets. Follow the instructions on the box or ask your pediatrician for the right dosage.

- **Children's ibuprofen.** I prefer ibuprofen (Motrin) to acetaminophen (Tylenol) as a fever reducer, simply because it works longer. Each dose is designed to last up to eight hours, versus Tylenol's four. If you're trying to keep a fever down at night, those extra four hours truly count. Also, ibuprofen is well suited for reducing swelling, perfect for all those eggs my toddlers got on their heads after they tripped and fell. Note: Both Motrin and Tylenol boxes recommend consulting a doctor for dosage information if your child is under two.

Natural Cold Remedies You Can Try

Cold medicines are no longer approved for children under six. If you relied on decongestants or antihistamines to make your toddler feel better, you're up the creek. Or are you?

Some folks have said that those multisymptom cold relievers really didn't help kids much at all. Herbalists, naturopaths, and ordinary moms have turned to natural remedies instead. Maybe some of these will help soothe your toddler:

- **Honey.** Honey beat out cough medicine as the best at relieving symptoms and aiding sleep when it comes to children's upper respiratory tracts, according to an *Archives of Pediatrics & Adolescents* study. (Note: Never give honey to a child under age one.)

- **Petroleum jelly.** Rub a little bit on your toddler's nose if it gets red and raw from all that snoogie wiping.

- **Cold air.** Every spring, my older son had a bout of croup— that barking cough caused by a virus that narrows the larynx. We tried to relieve his symptoms by sitting in a steam-filled bathroom, but that didn't work. For him, the best remedy was to lie by the open door, inhaling the cool evening air. If your toddler has croup, try both to see what works. If his breathing gets seriously impaired, however, rush him to the ER. We did once,

Okay, I admit it. . . .

"My son had the flu and we were not aware (no symptoms). We were in a discount store and thought someone had spilled apple juice in an aisle. It wasn't apple juice! He had diarrhea! None of the other shoppers even noticed. I was horrified and pretended it was apple juice."

—*Holly, Britt, Iowa*

and doctors put him on a ventilator with an inhaled steroid to open up his airways. Phew!

"I save some of my son's favorite DVDs for when he is sick. I set up the mini-DVD player on the arm of the sofa, and I put a chair with a sippy cup and some dry cereal where he can get it easily. The novelty of it all often distracts him, and any mess is easily cleaned up."

It worked for me!

—*Kellie, Derby, Connecticut*

How to Teach Your Toddler to Blow Her Nose

Can your toddler *bwow* her nose? I've read that toddlers are developmentally capable of blowing their noses by age two. Whether your toddler actually wants to blow her nose is another issue. Like anything else with toddlers, making a game of it helps them learn more quickly and easily. Here's how:

1. Teach her when her nose isn't all stuffed up. It'll make it easier for her to see the cause and effect of blowing out her nose.

2. First, teach her to blow through her mouth. You can blow out birthday candles or blow cotton balls across the coffee table.

3. Next, hold one of her nostrils and ask her to blow through her nose. Hold a ribbon or a strip of tissue under her nose, so she can see it blowing in the wind.

4. Then have her blow out one nostril into a tissue. Have her throw out the tissue and wash her hands (to help cut down on those twelve colds a year).

5. Reward her for blowing her nose with stickers, candy, whatever works for you.

6. Pat yourself on the back. Your toddler can blow her nose!

It worked for me!

"We call the advice nurse at our pediatrician's office so much that they know us by name. We rely on their advice for when to make an appointment with the pediatrician."

—Lee, San Jose, California

WE ASKED: How do you know when to call the doctor when your child is sick?

"I call if they are not sleeping, not playing very much, or the illness is just not going away in a reasonable amount of time."

—Julie, West Chester, Pennsylvania

Calling the Doctor: Good Idea or Neurotic Mother with Speed Dial?

WHENEVER I'M NOT sure if I should make an appointment with the pediatrician, I call the nurses' line and present my case. Then I call my mother, my mother-in-law, and any neighbor whose child has the same symptoms. I don't want to take my kids to a place where there are kids sicker than they are (and contagious), so I think long and hard about making that appointment.

Still, there are a few tried-and-true symptoms and signs that warrant that call.

When to Call the Doctor

- If your toddler's fever reaches 103 degrees Fahrenheit. You may be able to get her temperature down with ibuprofen, but you should call the doctor once her temp hits 103 or higher.

- If your toddler is wheezing or gasping. (For gasping, I'd rush to the ER.)

- If your toddler's cough gets worse, sounding wet or hacking over a day or two.

- If he's tugging or rubbing his ear. (It could be a sign of an ear infection.)

- If she's excessively tired or listless.

- If your toddler's cold symptoms get worse after five days or don't improve after ten. I could tell when my toddlers had sinus infections when their snoogies turned green. But I'm not a doctor, so make that call.

- She's not eating or her sleep is particularly poor for more than a day.

 WE ASKED: How do you know when to call the doctor when your child is sick?

> "If there seems to be pain of any kind, call. If you can make them laugh, don't worry, but call."
>
> —Kimberly, Slippery Rock, Pennsylvania

> "When she stops eating, that is a sure sign an ear infection has hit yet again!"
>
> —Leandra, Sumter, South Carolina

When to Keep Your Sick Toddler at Home

IT ALMOST SEEMS unfair, doesn't it? You're thinking of keeping your toddler home from day care, her playgroup, or her school *where she probably caught the darn cold in the first place.* You don't want your toddler to get everyone else sick, and yet you just know that half the kids there have runny noses anyhow. So how do you decide whether to sideline your sick toddler?

Some day care centers and schools have written rules about when a child can return after an illness. But for those places where you're just not sure what to do, here are some reasonable guidelines. Keep your toddler at home if:

- Your toddler has a fever, or for twenty-four hours after a fever. At my sons' school, a fever is defined as 100 degrees Fahrenheit or higher. While 98.6 degrees is considered normal, some children's temperatures run higher while others run lower. Learn your child's normal temperature, so you can better make your decision.

- Your toddler has diarrhea or is vomiting. If the vomiting stopped in the middle of the night, but she still seems queasy, keep her home.

- Your toddler has anything other than a cold that's still contagious. Ask your doctor about the contagiousness of your toddler's chicken pox, strep throat, scabies, lice, or various rashes. Some illnesses are no longer contagious after forty-eight hours of antibiotics treatment, while others have different criteria.

- You can afford to stay home. If you don't really have to be anywhere, why not let your toddler have another sick day at home with Mommy? If nothing else, it'll keep him from being exposed to other illnesses while his defenses are down, and you won't have to stuff your pockets full of tissues.

Will the Other Moms Hate You If Your Kid Is Sneezing?

You can cite all the pediatric advice you want, but the other moms at your playgroup probably aren't going to be too happy with you if you expose your sick toddler and his perpetually runny nose to all the other kids. Same goes for a one-on-one playdate. But before you cancel your plans, make a few phone calls to the other moms. There are many times my toddlers' playdates had colds, too, so we all just got together and sneezed a lot, like a TV commercial for Triaminic.

WE ASKED: Where do you get your toddler health information?

Our pediatrician: 70%
Common sense: 55%
Fellow moms: 55%
The Internet: 40%
Books: 25%
My mom/mother-in-law: 10%
Magazine articles: 10%

WE ASKED: How do you soothe your toddler when he or she is sick?

"An enormous amount of TV."

—Susan, Montville, New Jersey

Cranky Plus Preverbal Makes
for a Long Day

IT'S HARD ENOUGH getting anything done around the house when you've got a toddler underfoot, but when you've got a sick toddler, it's darn near impossible. She's sick, she's cranky, and she wants nothing to do with you and your desire to pay the bills or clean the kitchen floor. She wants Mommy, and she wants Mommy now! No, wait. . . . she wants *Dora the Explorer* on TV and a bowl full of Goldfish crackers. No, she wants her blankie. . . . This is going to be a long day.

The number-one rule when you have a sick toddler at home is to break all the rules. This isn't the time to enforce your "Only Thirty Minutes of TV" rule or your "Leave Mommy Alone While She Folds Laundry" rule. Tell your toddler you're having very special "Sick Day" rules, so she doesn't think that she'll get to snack on graham crackers all day long anytime, but only when her tummy's feeling a little funny.

It worked for me!

"My son went the entire first year of his life without even a sniffle. Then at a year and a half, he got hand-foot-mouth disease. He was miserable with a high fever and painful blisters for more than a week. Bending rules and making more time for them helps them through it. It also helps you keep your patience, which can wear pretty thin when you've been up for twenty hours holding your child."

—Kellie, Derby, Connecticut

WE ASKED: How do you soothe your toddler when he or she is sick?

"I get out their favorite DVDs, popsicles,
sports bottles with Gatorade, and pretty much wait
on them hand and foot. It's pretty glamorous."

—*Colleen, Tucson, Arizona*

When Mom Is Sick

YOU PROBABLY KNOW by now that moms don't get sick days. I used to be very happy when I came down with something on a Friday night, because it meant that I would be able to get a break while my husband was home from work over the weekend. But if you've got no back-up sitter and your toddler is home with you all day, you're in for an especially long day—or three. Here are some tricks for getting through your so-called sick day:

- **Postpone the videos.** Save the most sedentary activities for the afternoon when you're usually feeling your worst.

- **Don't stand.** Don't do any activities that require you to stand for long periods of time, such as baking or cleaning, or they'll only make you more tired. Stick to reading to your toddler, holding indoor picnics, playing with toys in one place, and so on.

- **Be the base.** Set up an activity where you are the home base, and therefore, don't leave the couch or bed. Send your toddler on a treasure hunt for various items in the same room. The more difficult the item is to find, the longer you'll get to rest your head on the pillow and dream of decongestants and bedtime.

• **Make a fort.** It'll keep everyone in one place so you don't get dizzy watching toddlers and their siblings. Read or make up stories or play with a quiet toy.

• **Movie time.** After ten hours of entertaining the kids with a box of tissues under your arm, you deserve to rest. Here are some particularly long videos to show your toddler. Yes, videos. They're just ninety minutes or so out of the 157,700 hours they get to be children:

> *Mary Poppins* (Rated G, 139 minutes)
> *Cars* (Rated G, 116 minutes)
> *Finding Nemo* (Rated G, 100 minutes)
> *Charlotte's Web—1973 version* (Rated G, 94 minutes)
> *Ice Age* (Rated PG, 90 minutes)
> *Madagascar* (Rated PG, 86 minutes)
> *The Little Mermaid* (Rated G, 83 minutes)
> *Toy Story* (Rated G, 81 minutes)

WE ASKED: What kinds of tricks do you have to get some TLC when you're sick and caring for a toddler at the same time?

"I lose all expectations of getting anything done (cooking, cleaning, and so on). I just focus on resting however I can. If you know anyone who likes to cook for you, take them up on it. Just return the favor when you can. You will be surprised how many people feel your pain and want to help."

—*Anne, West Milford, New Jersey*

Gimme a break

Train Your Kids to Watch TV Shows That You Like

When you're under the weather, watching *Caillou* may just make you feel worse. Train your toddler to watch—or at least let you watch—TV shows that are toddler friendly, such as *Ellen*, some *Mythbusters* episodes, and most HGTV and Food Network shows.

Just a minute!

The Best Laid Plans: Your So-Called Sick Day

- ~~Sleep in late.~~
- Get up at 5:30 to explain to my precocious two-year-old why it's still dark out even though it's technically morning.
- ~~Eat a healthful breakfast.~~
- Shove toast crusts, apple peels, and juice swill down my throat while trying to keep up with a toddler who is heading for our new plasma TV with a plastic sword and an attitude.
- ~~Watch *Ellen*.~~
- Watch *Caillou*—four times in a row, glad that my stuffy head is muffling his very annoying, sickly sweet voice just enough.
- ~~Take conference call about hot new initiative at work.~~
- Call pediatrician about hot new fever toddler is now running.
- ~~Watch the noon news.~~
- Watch *Caillou*—four times in a row in waiting area for pediatrician, who says my toddler's fever is "just teething."
- ~~Nap.~~
- Watch toddler nap in backseat of car just long enough to feel refreshed, thereby staying up the entire rest of the day and well into the night.
- ~~Check e-mail.~~
- Play "Spell with Caillou" online game—four times in a row.
- ~~Heat up soup for dinner.~~
- Clean up soup that toddler, um, revisited. (Teething, my butt, doc. It's a stomach flu!)
- ~~Watch evening news.~~
- Wish I could watch *Caillou* instead of preparing for the long night ahead, caring for a sick toddler. Oh, and for my own flu, too.

Chapter Thirteen

But What About . . . ?
Extra Help for Parents of Multiples, Stay-at-Home Moms, Starting Day Care, and Other Special Situations

> "I work three evenings a week teaching and tutoring, so my husband gives them dinner and baths and does the bedtime routine with them."
>
> —Anne, West Milford, New Jersey

It worked for me!

Outside the Box

Every morning, I drove my three-year-old to preschool and then rushed to get things done with my toddler in tow. I knew I only had a few hours until the pain would get so unbearable that I'd have to lie down while a sitter watched my kids.

I had endometriosis, a chronic disease of the pelvis that caused me a great deal of pain and fatigue. While the other mommies were planning their afternoons at the playground, I was counting down to my first dose of Percocet for the day. Funny, I don't remember anyone mentioning parenting around pain at my baby shower.

One day, frustrated that I couldn't get any doctors to take me seriously, I broke down in tears—in front of my kids. My three-year-old offered to help me even though my doctors wouldn't. To this day, he remembers that moment. And so do I.

Not all parenting situations fit neatly into boxes. From at-home motherhood, which is less common than in our mothers' day, to divorce, to parenting multiples, there are all sorts of situations that make parenting your toddler all the more challenging. I'll touch on some of the most common situations, some of which I've experienced myself, and offer up five tips for each.

WE ASKED: What surprised you most about parenting a toddler?

"How busy it is."

—*Alexis, Marysville, California*

Stay-at-Home Motherhood

THOUGH THERE ARE some 7 million full-time stay-at-home mothers, not all of them live in your neighborhood, and so, sometimes it can be downright lonely being a stay-at-home mother, especially when half the neighbors are at work all day. But it can also be rewarding and fun. It's all in how you look at it.

Five Tips for Staying Home with Your Toddler

1. **Get the heck out of the house.** Join a playgroup or hang out at the park. Whatever you do, find a way to get out and about with your toddler several days a week so that you have grown-ups to talk to. Also, join a mother's group or set up nights out with friends or hubby, so you can dress up and go out without a diaper bag over your shoulder or fingerprints on your shirt.

2. **Back off.** Just because you can stay home doesn't mean you have to make every waking moment of your toddler's life enriching and educational. He needs to learn how to entertain himself, and you need to sit and read a magazine with a cup of coffee now and then. He'll become more independent, and you'll be more relaxed.

3. **Enlist hubby.** When you're a stay-at-home mom, it's easy to fall into the trap of "This is my job!" and, therefore, feel you have to do everything. But staying home with a toddler is a 100-hour-a-week job, plus you're on call all night. Get your husband to help out as much as possible, because an exhausted wife can be a lousy wife.

4. **Keep a schedule.** While an aimless day is refreshing now and then, it's important to keep a schedule so that your days have some structure. It will not only make your long days

feel less overwhelming, it will also teach your toddler to expect meals, naps, and bedtime at regular times, thereby cutting down on tantrums. A schedule also helps prepare your toddler for preschool.

Okay, I admit it. . . .

"No matter how disciplined you are, how structured your routine is, a toddler has a mind of their own!"

—*Michelle, Sarasota, Florida*

5. **Have something of your own.** If you make every moment of every day all about your toddler, you'll burn out. You need something that's all your own. Join a gym that offers child care, take up a hobby, such as scrapbooking or wine making, or set up a regular Girls Night Out with your friends—no kids allowed.

Working from Home

IT WAS THE first time I was working with a real live New York City editor on the phone. She was making suggestions for some changes to an essay she was considering publishing in her magazine, and I was pretending this sort of thing happened all the time. My toddler, on the other hand, was insisting that I make birthday cakes out of Play-Doh. Every time I put the Play-Doh down, he started to fuss. Finally, the editor said, "I hear little ones. Is this a bad time to call?" With toddlers in the house, there is no good time to call. That's why the good Lord invented e-mail. Ah, but I was stuck—

also, very good at making Play-Doh cakes with one hand while typing with the other and holding the phone with my shoulder.

Five Tips for Working at Home with Your Toddler Underfoot

1. **Carve out your work space.** You might be able to work on your laptop surrounded by Legos, but should you? Not really. You need to create your own this-is-Mommy's-job work space, whether it's in a spare bedroom or a hutch in the family room. Your work space is not a play place. Let your kids know it, and you'll get more done.

2. **Be flexible.** You might have big work plans for nap time, but your toddler might decide to skip the nap and hang out with you all afternoon. Be prepared to shift your work hours to nighttime or weekends when your toddler's plans for you change.

3. **Get help.** Hire a sitter or trade mornings with a neighbor who has a toddler. Do what it takes to make sure you have the time you need to work from home without driving yourself crazy. You'll get more done quickly when you can concentrate on work, rather than making Play-Doh cakes.

4. **Take work seriously.** Never refer to your job or business as a "hobby," even if it doesn't make much money. The more respect you have for your work, the more your family will help you make sure you have the time to get to your desk.

5. **Spread the word.** You never know if one of your neighbors could use your services or products, or if they're hiring people to work from home. Make sure you network, even if it's at Mommy & Me, because you could get work out of it.

Starting Day Care or Preschool

WITH MOST MOTHERS working outside the house, many toddlers are in day care. Others start preschool as young as age two. Whether you need the hours to work or your toddler needs more structured socialization, day care or preschool might be right for your family. But sending your little one off for a few hours or the entire day requires research, planning, and organization. How can you make sure you're selecting the right day care center or preschool for your toddler?

Five Tips for Choosing Day Care or Preschool

1. **See for yourself.** Ask for a tour of the facility—without your toddler—during operating hours. You don't want to bring your toddler along until you've chosen your facility. Take note of how the adults interact with the children and whether the toddlers seem content or anxious.

2. **Ask questions.** Don't be afraid to ask a lot of questions. You need to feel completely comfortable leaving your toddler there. Some questions to consider include: Do you have an open-door policy for parents? Is the center registered with

the state? and What is your policy for sick children? Also, ask about the adult-child ratio. Experts recommend no more than eight toddlers per adult.

3. **Take a close look at the activities and games.** Make sure that the toys are clean and age appropriate. See if there are set activities that your toddler would enjoy. Find out if the center encourages activity so that your toddler isn't sitting around all day. Ask whether they go outside, weather permitting, and check out the playground.

4. **Interview other parents.** You'll get the inside scoop from parents who currently send their toddlers to the facility, as well as from those whose children are "graduates." Make sure you interview parents who left the facility as well. They might have a reason that's important to you.

5. **Determine their philosophy.** Do they offer a "learn through play" environment or a more structured Montessori-type school? Matching the center's philosophy to your toddler's temperament takes some research, but it's worth the effort.

My, Oh My, Oh My: Three Toddlers?

ACCORDING TO THE National Center for Health Statistics, the twin birth rate has risen 55 percent since 1980. Triplets and quadruplets are on the rise, too, and at least one set of parents of sextuplets (and twins!) has their own reality TV show, *Jon and Kate*

Plus 8, which has more drama and peril than *Desperate House-wives*. Even if you don't have cameras following you around, parenting more than one toddler at a time has got to be harried and, at times, exhausting. I don't have multiples (though I did have two toddlers under the same roof), so I'll let MommaSaid's moms of multiples supply the tips.

Five Tips for Parenting Multiple Toddlers

1. **Keep multiple stuff.** "It is a good idea to keep two or three of everything." —Marlena, Harriman, Tennessee

2. **Synchronize schedules.** "Get them to nap at the same time!" —Stacy, Fort Wayne, Indiana

3. **Treat them like individuals.** "You cannot treat your twins the same. They are two different people with minds of their own. The only good thing is I am only going through these stages *once*." —Judy, New Milford, New Jersey

4. **Contain them.** "Containment is one of the secrets to surviving little twins—exersaucers, swings, gates in every doorway, and a really sturdy double stroller. I kept using my stroller until their feet were dragging on the ground." —Joyce, Minneapolis, Minnesota

5. **Don't referee.** "With twins, it's always like having a playdate in your house, twenty-four hours a day. When my girls would fight over something, I would automatically take it away and put it on top on the fridge if they couldn't work it

out. That way I cut down on the fights." —Jill, Kinnelon, New Jersey

Daddy's Deployed

YOUR HUSBAND IS deployed overseas with the military, and you're at home tending to the kids and life and a toddler who misses her daddy. It's just not the same as having a husband who travels a lot. You're going solo and handling extra issues other moms can't begin to understand. I searched the Internet to find the top tips on handling the stress of parenting while your spouse is deployed.

Five Tips for Holding Down the Fort When Hubby's Overseas

1. **Avoid watching the news.** If you find yourself tuned into CNN in the wee hours of the night, worrying about your husband being in harm's way, you're only going to make yourself a wreck—and your toddler will sense it. Stick to the good news that comes from hearing from your spouse when he calls or e-mails you.

2. **Make Daddy known.** Some toddlers have never met or have forgotten their deployed fathers. Make sure you keep photos of Daddy around the house and talk about him a lot. Have your toddler get on the phone with him, even if the conversation makes absolutely no sense. That way, he won't seem like a stranger to your toddler when he returns home.

3. **Skip the videos.** Toddlers might not understand why Daddy can't come out of the TV and hang out with them. (That's why they talk to Joe on *Blue's Clues* as though he's in the living room.) Limit home videos unless your toddler understands Daddy's not in the television.

4. **Keep in touch.** If your husband's schedule permits it, try to set up a regular time to talk, and make a big deal out of when he calls. Your toddler will come to understand that Daddy is so loved, everyone celebrates when he calls.

5. **Don't show your fear.** Your toddler is too young to understand that Daddy might be in harm's way. Save your sad feelings for adults who can help you work through your emotions.

After Separation and Divorce

SOME 20 MILLION children will be raised by single parents. Certainly, you're not alone if you are separated or divorced, though you might feel like it. Explaining to a toddler why Daddy doesn't live with you anymore is complicated and difficult. I've searched for some of the best tips for handling the situation.

Five Tips for Parenting a Toddler After Divorce

1. **Don't refer to Daddy as "Bonehead."** No matter how you feel about your ex right now, don't share it with your kids. Keep your bad feelings about Daddy to yourself when the kids are around.

2. **Keep things as routine as possible.** Try to limit the amount of change your toddler endures while she adjusts to her new family structure. Keep her playgroup, school, house, and schedule as similar as possible at this tumultuous time in her life.

3. **Don't play fairy godmother.** Now isn't the time to let go of the rules and cater to your toddler's every whim. Even if Daddy is buying her pretty pink tricycles and trips to Disney World, resist the urge to compete. She needs structure and boundaries just as much now as she did before the divorce.

4. **Don't ask your toddler to play favorites.** It isn't fair to your child to make him pick you over your ex for anything, including visitation schedules and love. Let him treat the both of you the way he wants to.

5. **Let go of the hostility.** If your ex is ten minutes late dropping off your toddler, let it go. You don't need to turn every little transgression into a battle zone. The more realistic and relaxed you are, the better it is for your toddler.

It worked for me!

"I beg my husband to stay home from work and help me with the kids."

—*Whitney, Bridgewater, Virginia*

Mommy's Sick

IT'S ONE THING to take care of a toddler when you have the flu and quite another when you have a chronic disease, such as multiple sclerosis or cancer. I've parented through chronic pain from endometriosis and the six surgeries that went with it, and lymphoma, so I know firsthand how nerve-wracking it can be when you're a mom who's chronically ill. Here are a few pointers:

Five Tips for Parenting a Toddler When You're Chronically Ill

1. **Let go of the old you.** Before you were sick, no doubt you could get a whole lot more done than you can now. But running yourself into the ground while you try to be Perfect Mommy doesn't do anyone any good. Let go of the old you and learn to parent as the new you. It's better for you, your health, and your toddler.

2. **Call in reinforcements to maintain the status quo.** Ask relatives, neighbors, and friends to help care for your toddler so you can rest. I learned that when you're seriously ill, people want to help and there's nothing wrong with asking for it. The more your toddler can keep his usual schedule, the better it'll help him adjust to your illness.

3. **Hug and kiss a lot.** Your toddler needs it, and so do you. Showing affection to your toddler helps reassure her that Mommy's still Mommy, no matter how funny she looks when she's bald from chemo.

4. **Save the outings for the good days.** If you have a burst of energy, take your toddler out to the park, the mall, or the backyard—whatever you can handle. But don't make any promises ahead of time. If your toddler knows your illness keeps him home, he'll start to resent it.

Okay, I admit it. . . .

"Hearing her say 'I love you, too, Mommy' with a big hug and kiss is just the best!"

—*Leandra,*
Sumter, South Carolina

5. **Give your toddler as much attention as you can.** You don't have to host a tea party or play Follow the Leader to be a good mom. Your toddler just wants your time and attention. Play quiet games or watch a video while snuggling on the couch.

Which One of These Is Not Like the Others?

WHATEVER YOUR SPECIAL situation, seek out other people who are going through or who have been through the same thing as you. You'll feel much better when you can share your concerns and issues with someone who truly understands what it's like to be in your shoes. On the Internet, you'll find websites that offer support both online and in person, and there are lots of books about your specific issue on the shelves. If you need one-on-one help with a serious issue, consider seeing a trained counselor. Whatever you do, remember that your toddler loves you no matter what.

Momma Said

WE ASKED: What do you wish someone had told you about parenting toddlers?

"Your life is all consumed. You will never have time for yourself. But that wouldn't have mattered because I wouldn't change it for the world."

—*Jennifer, Flemington, New Jersey*

Gimme a break

Start Your Own Home-Based Business

One way to get some "me time" without leaving the house is to start your own home-based business. There are numerous resources to help you get started, but one of the best is to talk to other moms who have started their own businesses with toddlers underfoot. You can find them online or right in your own neighborhood.

Just a minute!

WHAT I MISS MOST . . .

. . . using my tweezers on my eyebrows, instead of using them to retrieve Barbie's shoes from the heating grate.

. . . dreaming long enough to find out whether George Clooney wears boxers or briefs.

. . . having an entire conversation that has nothing to do with poop. Aw, geez! There it is again.

. . . accessorizing with jewelry and scarves, rather than marker and what appears to be apple sauce.

. . . dashing out with just a small purse and some lip gloss, instead of packing up like the traveling circus just to go to the mall.

. . . showering without someone handing me the phone and saying, "Some wady wants to tawk to you."

. . . reading a book anywhere but my minivan, because my two-year-old naps only in his car seat.

. . . reaching the bottom of the laundry pile.

. . . my purse, which I haven't seen since I bought the diaper bag.

. . . sitting for longer than it takes to pee.

Bye-Bye!

So, there you have it—everything I would tell you about parenting toddlers if we met at the back fence. I hope you got a lot out of all the mom-tested tips, the "been there" stories, and the much-needed, reassuring pats on the back.

Whether you have troubles potty training, spend your days pulling a toddler down off the furniture, or you're just plain exhausted, remember: you're not the only one going through it, no matter how lonely it feels at times.

Okay, I admit it. . . .

"It's a lot of work, but it's okay to relax and just let them be."

—*Emmie,
Utica, New York*

Whenever you need a pick-me-up, advice, or something to read that doesn't rhyme, flip through this guide or drop by MommaSaid.net for laughs and validation. We're here for you, no matter what your toddler is up to now.

Just a minute!

Toddlerhood Exit Interview

1. What is your primary reason for leaving?

   My toddler starts preschool tomorrow. Besides, a girl can only take a year or two of pulling her kid down from the shelves at Target while old ladies look on and shake their heads.

2. Did anything trigger your decision to leave?

   Yes. Successful potty training and the freedom that comes with it. Also, the lure of two-and-a-half whole hours to myself, three mornings a week. (See above about preschool. Also, shelves at Target.)

3. What was most satisfying part of toddlerhood?

   The part where she started calling me "Momma" and stopped referring to everything else as "Dada." Because, frankly, it gets old hearing about Dada Dada Dada Dada all day long when Dada doesn't even get home until seven and has no clue what size Pull-Ups to buy.

4. What was the least satisfying part of toddlerhood?

   Nobody cares if you know the Spanish word for "bridge" before Dora says it

5. Did your duties turn out as you expected?

If somebody had told me that I'd carry my kid by his overall straps just to be safe in the parking lot, set up a barricade that Homeland Security would be proud of to keep my toddler in his room at night, or change poopy diapers in the middle of our playgroup—while he was standing up and singing "I use my body when I have to poop"—I wouldn't have believed it anyhow.

6. Did you receive enough training to do your job well?

See above. How can you train for that? In the army? The circus? Prison?

7. Did you receive adequate feedback about your performance?

Sure, if you count the time my toddler yelled across the library after Story Time ended: "Mommy! You didn't forget to come back for me today!"

8. Can we do anything to encourage you to stay?

Nope. I've already been roped into being room mother for my kid's preschool class. Besides, they're not called the "Terrific Twos." I'm done . . . for now, anyhow.

Index